Roads to Recovery

Roads to Recovery

Inspiring stories from survivors of illness, accident and loss

Pamela Traynor

ALLEN & UNWIN

Copyright © Pamela Traynor, 1997

All rights reserved. No part of this book may be reproduced or transmitted in any form or by any means, electronic or mechanical, including photocopying, recording or by any information storage and retrieval system, without prior permission in writing from the publisher.

Photograph on p. 112 of Christina Brock is courtesy of News Limited.

First published in 1997 by
Allen & Unwin
9 Atchison Street
St Leonards NSW 2065
Australia
Phone: (61 2) 9901 4088
Fax: (61 2) 9906 2218
E-mail: frontdesk@allen-unwin.com.au
URL: http://www.allen-unwin.com.au

National Library of Australia
Cataloguing-in-Publication entry:

Roads to recovery: inspiring stories from survivors of
  illness, accident and loss

  ISBN 1 86448 195 1.

  1. Sick—Psychology. 2. Accidents—Psychological aspects.
  3. Loss (Psychology). I. Traynor, Pamela, 1941- .

155.916

Set in 10.5/12 pt Sabon by DOCUPRO, Sydney
Printed by Australian Print Group, Maryborough, Vic.

10 9 8 7 6 5 4 3 2 1

For my daughter, Jessica

'Come to the edge,' he said
They said, 'We are afraid'.
'Come to the edge,' he said
They came.
He pushed them . . .
And they flew.

Guillaume Apollinaire

Contents

PART I   ACCIDENT
1 Mark Bagshaw   3
2 Janine Shepherd   31
3 Allana Arnot   56
4 Alex Blaszczynski, *Associate Professor and
   Deputy Director, Psychiatry Research and
   Teaching Unit, University of New South Wales*   76

PART II   ILLNESS
5 Kerry Harfield   87
6 Barbara Asgill   100
7 Christina Brock   112
8 Stewart Dunn, *Professor of Psychological
   Medicine, Royal North Shore Hospital and
   University of Sydney*   125
9 Ian Hickie, *Associate Professor of Psychiatry,
   University of New South Wales; Director,
   Academic Department of Psychiatry,
   St George Hospital*   137
10 Simon Champ   145
11 Rosemary Lorz   166
12 Alan Rosen, *Director, Royal North Shore
   Hospital and Community Adult Mental Health
   Services; Associate Professor and Clinical Senior
   Lecturer, Universities of Sydney and Wollongong*   192

CONTENTS

PART III LOSS

13 Zalmai Haidary   205
14 Margaret Cunningham, *Executive Director,
    Service for the Treatment and Rehabilitation
    of Torture and Trauma Survivors* (STARTTS)   230
15 Lynne Bon De Veire   236
16 Dianne McKissock, *Director, Bereavement
    Care Centre*   264

Introduction

It was when a close family member was involved in a road accident that I thought of writing this book as I experienced first hand her slow and painful road to full recovery.

I needed to find out about the theories and what seemed to be the mystery surrounding recovery. What were the determining factors and characteristics which enabled some people to recover from a serious illness, accident or loss? When a tragic event threatens to diminish or end a person's life, why is it that, despite a pessimistic prognosis, some not only survive and recover, but go on to thrive and to lead an even richer and fulfilling existence than before the crisis? If we were to examine separate individuals with similar profiles, who share the same medical history, state of health, age, social support, medical intervention at the time of injury or diagnosis of disease, why is it that one will recover while another dies? Is it genetic predisposition, optimistic personality type, or simply good luck? And what causes disease to develop? What role does stress play?

To attempt to discover some answers, I went on a journey to interview people who have recovered from trauma of various kinds; I sought medical, psychiatric and psychological opinion and discovered a mountain of studies, both Australian and international. Health psychology and immuno-psychology are booming. There are thousands of studies concerning cancer and the implication of

INTRODUCTION

personality and behaviour. Many studies attempt to find a relationship between personality types and heart attack—'the coronary prone personality'—or stress as a factor in the development of cancer, and behaviour modification in prevention and recovery. The psychological studies are in conflict and some of them have led to a 'blame the victim' conclusion—the view that if your attitude to your disease or disability isn't positive enough, you won't survive.

This collection is not a comprehensive account of why some people recover from a serious trauma or disease while others don't, but it raises important questions and offers some insights. Although the only certain prediction we can make about life is that it must end, when and how may provide other perspectives. That turns my attention to the analogy of the lifeboat, told to me by Professor Stewart Dunn.

If a ship capsizes or a plane crashes into the ocean and you think about the people who survive that experience, a number of factors will affect them.

'There are a number of environmental factors, some of which are within your control, some of which are beyond your control,' says Stewart Dunn. 'If you happen to land in the water and you have food in your pocket, because you were smart enough to grab some food when you heard the plane or boat was going down, then that increases your chances of survival.

'If you were lucky enough—which has nothing to do with factors in your control—to land near a piece of timber or a lifeboat rather than 300 metres away, then that increases your odds of survival, but that's more or less a chance factor. And maybe it matters where you were in the plane when it went down. So there are environmental and other chance factors which increase the odds of your survival which have nothing to do with your psychology.

'You and ten other people might be left clinging to a

INTRODUCTION

piece of fuselage. Perhaps a hungry shark swims past and attacks one in the group rather than you, so all the environmental factors have been taken care of and the personal control factors—in terms of having a bit of food or tying yourself onto the fuselage with a piece of rope—have all been accounted for. What you then have left is the psychological–biological factor.

'Out of those ten people, after four days adrift at sea with nothing to eat or drink and the sun burning down, perhaps eight will say, "I can't hang on any more, it's too much. I'm prepared to let go and die". So they make a conscious decision to let go. It doesn't matter any more, they don't care enough any more to stay there.

'Then you have two people who say, "No matter what, I'm not going to give up while there is a cell alive in my body. I'm going to cling to this fuselage because something will happen, a boat will come . . ." And I think there is something in that notion, "something will happen", that makes people hang on. And there is something in believing nothing is going to change that allows people to slip away. I think that is supported by the studies of survivors of holocaust and other situations where people have been under severe duress.

'My reading of that literature is that the people who survived things like the Holocaust, the concentration camps, the POWs in Germany during the war, is that one of the characteristics that seems to stand out in the reports is a belief that it will get better, it will pass, it will finish. And as long as you've got that belief, then you've got something. You want a reason for fighting.'

Whatever reasons can be discerned in the recovery stories told here, the people dealt with trauma in their own individual ways and the common thread is that of extraordinary determination. Perhaps it is that determination we may all learn from in our everyday lives when we face personal obstacles, both large and small. And perhaps their stories can also inspire us, in a wider context, to

INTRODUCTION

deal with large-scale problems which require similar levels of determination and courage.

Finally, it has not been possible to include all those I interviewed, simply because of limitations of length, but I am grateful to all of them for recounting their very personal stories, their insights and specialist knowledge so generously. A special thanks as well to all the experts who accepted stoically that only a summarised account of what they told me could be included.

Acknowledgements

I am indebted to my editor Nina Riemer for her support, meticulous professionalism and good humour. As well, my gratitude to my son, Tom, who so patiently assisted me when my deadline was looming. And to Christopher Bowen, a kindred spirit.

PART I
ACCIDENT

1

Mark Bagshaw

When Mark was sixteen years old, a diving accident left him with Level C5/6 quadriplegia (complete) resulting in limited movement in his arms and no movement at all in his fingers.

By the time we met, his reputation as a highly successful forty-year-old business executive had preceded him. I was expecting to find a rather hard-bitten stereotype of a business man, but a remarkably different person emerged during the course of our meetings and subsequent friendship.

ACCIDENT

You were sixteen when you had the accident which was to change your life. Can you take me back to before that time?

My young life was very standard I'd have to say. I lived in the south-western suburbs of Sydney in a stable sort of family with Mum and Dad and my sister. I have very fond memories of family life, and I did all the sorts of things that normal kids did.

I was involved in a bit of sport but don't know that I was particularly good at it. I think that the things I was least good at were the things I liked the most—like soccer. I used to love soccer, but I was hopeless at it. Absolutely dreadful! I spent most of my time, if I got on the field at all, as the 'orange boy'—playing fullback when we knew there was virtually no chance of the other team getting the ball anywhere near the other end of the field. Or as a forward if we knew that defence was going to be the way to win the game. So I was not considered to be the most valuable asset to the soccer team. But I used to love it.

I played tennis, but I used to get bad tempered and angry if I hit the ball out. Angry with myself. I've always been a bit of a perfectionist, I guess. I'd get angry with myself if I wasn't performing as well as I should have. And I did some running and various other sports. I did quite well at schoolwork but, as my mother was always saying, nowhere near as well as I probably could have. She was right. I know I never applied myself to study as much as I should have. My report cards all said the same thing and always used to irritate me—I was always near the top of the class, but rarely ever at the top. I hated study anyway.

I've always liked learning things if I can apply them in practical terms very quickly. I found that if study was leading perhaps to employment some time in the future, that in itself was not enough motivation. It was the same for me at university. But when I started working with IBM and spent the first twelve months studying intensely, more intensely than I've ever studied in my life, the next day I was applying the skills that I'd learnt. And that was satisfying. I would spend inordinate amounts of time studying and did very well at that because it had a practical application straight away.

I'd always thought that I'd either be a doctor or an engineer. But the only thing that I ever really shone at when I was younger was music. I started learning music early, from the age of about six I learned the piano. I was studying for my AMusA, a diploma in music, when I was injured. At that age I was reasonably advanced and I studied a number of other instruments not quite up to the same level—flute, guitar and other stringed instruments. I've always loved music. It's probably the greatest love of my life. But I'm not sure that I would have chosen it as a career. It was more a central part of my life, and still is. That was one thing where I really felt I excelled and I also felt that it gave me more personal rewards than anything else I did. I could sit for hours and just play the piano and love it. I spent an enormous amount of time listening to music. But apart from that I struggled to find anything else that I was very good at. I wasn't heavily involved in student politics at university. I was more interested in girls at that stage.

The day of the accident. Can you recall that day?
It was an ordinary day. We were up on the Central Coast. Mum and Dad had a holiday house and we used to go up there quite a lot. It was Easter Monday. I've got clear enough memories of it. I was up there with Mum and Dad and my sister and a friend of hers, and a girlfriend.

We woke up that morning and Dad was quite sick with hay fever; he really needed to go to hospital he was so bad. So I drove the car over to Avoca Beach—Dad used to let me drive up there even though I was under age. I drove to the beach with the family and the three girls. It

ACCIDENT

was a hot day, swimming weather. Mum and Dad then went into Gosford Hospital and so they left us there. The four of us were on the beach and I just got up, ran down the beach and dived into the water. It was too shallow. I hit my head on the bottom. The sand didn't drop away under the water as quickly as I thought it would. So I dived in, hit my head and broke my neck.

I recall floating on top of the surface, but face down, and I couldn't move anything at all. I was completely paralysed. I was completely unable to move. I had my eyes open. I could see the bottom. I don't know that I would have drowned but I could have come close to needing resuscitation had it not been for the fact that I'd taken a very deep breath before I dived in. And I'd done that because I had good lung capacity from playing wind instruments and I'd also done lifesaving and had done a fair bit of swimming, so I had good breath control. I held onto that deep breath for an extended period of time. I'd always played around with it. I used to swim the length of the Olympic pool and make a bit of a thing of swimming under water. If you hold your breath for a long time you get that feeling that you're desperate to take a breath but if you hold your breath long enough, that goes away.

I don't think anybody knew what had happened. There were a lot of people on the beach but it took them a while to twig that this person wasn't moving. So I had to hold on for quite some time. I recall that I was just about to take a breath, I just couldn't do it any longer, when I saw these feet running into the water directly behind me. So I held on for a fraction longer and they pulled me out. There was a doctor on the beach and he started to give very clear instructions to the lifesavers not to move me and how to put me on a stretcher.

I didn't know what the problem was, and I didn't have this strong sense of fear about it. Once I was taken out of the water I knew I was safe enough. I wasn't in any pain. I had no feeling or sensation. I couldn't move but I didn't go into panic. They took me into the first-aid room at the surf club until the ambulance came and in the interim my parents had come back and Dad was then with me.

They put me into an ambulance and obviously this doctor knew what the problem was because he insisted I had to be taken to Royal North Shore Hospital in Sydney rather than the local hospital.

I was in the emergency unit for two weeks. There were X-rays taken but I found out later that they knew immediately how serious the damage was. And they pretty well knew that it was going to be permanent. They judged that by the amount of blood in my spinal cord. If all the nerves are severed then they bleed. They told Mum and Dad very early how serious it was but they didn't tell me straight away. They told me they didn't know how bad it would be until spinal shock had worn off.

In my case the bones went straight back into place again, so I didn't need traction, they just put a collar around my neck and kept me very still until the bones knit again. But the damage had been done to the spinal cord, it was completely severed.

If you look at a chart of the spinal column and the central nervous system, showing where the nerves to all the peripherals come from and where they go to, you could read off exactly whether I'd be able to move by the chart. It was a complete fracture. Some spinal cord injuries are what's called 'incomplete'. That means that not all of the nerves in the spinal cord are severed at the point of the injury and therefore there can sometimes be partial or even full recovery. These are the cases which are often seen as 'miracles' by the popular press. Mine wasn't like that—all the nerves in my spinal cord were severed. I was quadriplegic.

During the ten months I spent in the hospital I had a lot of visitors, particularly in the early days, but right

ACCIDENT

throughout I had a fairly constant group of visitors—family, friends, people from school. I always looked forward to seeing people—their support was always valuable and, let's face it, it relieved some of the boredom. And part of each day I spent misbehaving in one way or another. I remember being particularly fond of the electric wheelchairs they had in the spinal unit and one day taking off in an electric chair out of the hospital grounds and up the Pacific Highway with two nurses in hot pursuit. The batteries finally went flat . . . that's how the nurses caught me.

Who actually told you about your injuries?

The doctors talked to me about it. But before they talked to me, I'd reached conclusions during this two-week period in the emergency unit. Even though I'd been told that spinal shock was still in effect, I'd reached the conclusion that I wasn't getting anywhere with my back. They talked more about exactly what had happened and the type of fractures. I remember thinking that I wasn't going to waste any time in holding out false hopes that I'd get movement back. I remember even as early as my first few days in the hospital starting to think about how I'd be in a wheelchair.

It was pretty clear what the outcome was going to be. They explained, 'If it's a complete fracture you won't be able to walk'. The reality of that didn't really sink in until later on. But it was clear that I was going to need to use a wheelchair for the rest of my life. And I thought, well, there must be ways I can overcome the effects of that. It must have been the larrikin in me, perhaps, but I recall thinking, this could be good fun, roaring around the corridors of the hospital and then roaring around the corridors of the school . . . or wherever. I don't know why but it just never really daunted me all that much. I just worked it out logically. I thought, If I'm going to go somewhere that's upstairs, then I'll get people to carry me up the stairs. You know, that's not rocket science, you don't need to be a genius to work that one out.

But I remember thinking, well, I'll go back to school . . . and I thought through the layout of the school which wasn't particularly accessible. I remembered what my days had been like before the accident and I wondered how I'd undertake my English class from nine o'clock to eleven and then my Maths class and so on. I knew where the stairs were, and where my classrooms were so it was a case of working out how to get to them. And I decided, well, this is how I'll do it—I'll get somebody to lift me up there. In the end, though, they changed the classrooms around and it worked out.

Do you think it's easier to adjust to a disability when you're at the age you were at the time of your accident?

I don't know that it is age. I don't think it's got a great deal to do with age at all, actually. I don't know that I can comment generally about disability, because I've only had that sort of intense, direct experience with a traumatic spinal cord injury, which obviously has some specific aspects. As a general comment, I'd say that from what I've observed, the vast majority of people who experience serious traumatic accidents like this don't cope very well with it—even statistics will bear that out.

What makes you different? Why did you cope better?

I think for a couple of reasons. I've thought about this a lot because I've been asked a lot—particularly in the last few years—Why have you been able to do the things you're doing? And I think basically the disability is irrelevant. It's not irrelevant to my life, it's ridiculous to say that, but it's irrelevant to my participation in a normal sort of lifestyle these days. It's irrelevant to my progress at work. It's irrelevant to what I do socially.

ACCIDENT

At the time of the accident, in that twelve months after, were they your feelings? 'I'm going to be able to get on with my life in the same way'?

Yes. And that's a clear memory from very early on—the first few days. When I think back now and ask why I felt that way about it when I now know that most people feel differently, the answer is that I've just always been like that. It's my personality. It's just the way I approach things.

Like what? Optimistic, positive, determined?

Yes. Very driven. Very motivated. Very dogmatic. I think there are always opposite sides to every coin, and there are definitely opposite sides to my coin. For example, the things that sustained me during the earlier times of my disability, are some of the things that were also negatives when it came to the break-up of my marriage. My being self-centred and dogmatic and so on. In that sense bad traits when it comes to that aspect of life, but positive things in coping with the disability which was something very personal and something that required a lot of energy and motivation.

In that twelve months or so afterwards, did you think about how the accident would effect your relationship with girls?

I guess to some extent I did, yes. It's not a silly statement exactly, but I'm sure some people would wonder why, given that it obviously has such an impact physically—that I'm in a wheelchair—I never lost my positive body image. I just didn't. Perhaps it was naive to think that I would somehow be any less attractive than I was previously but that's the way I felt. And of course, it was a very interesting time. I was sixteen. I was in hospital and at that time the nurses were primarily trainee nurses about my age, so I'd have to say that I didn't come out of hospital feeling that this was going to be a disaster.

What sort of support did you receive after the accident?

I had tremendous support from the community generally. An example most vivid in my mind is the support that I gained immediately from my school. The headmaster and the chaplain came in the next day and said to me and to Mum and Dad, 'Forget about any issues you might have about Mark coming back to school. We will fix the problem. End of story.' And they also said to Mum and Dad, 'You'll have some financial challenges during the next year, we'll waive the school fees'. It was a private school.

That sort of support was incredibly valuable and removed a major obstacle, because getting an education was the most important thing that was happening in my life at that stage. To have the school say, 'We are here to support you, and we will fix these problems; we'll overcome them no matter how we have to do it'—you can't estimate how much of a positive impact that had. And the other group that was incredibly supportive a little bit later was the Commonwealth Rehabilitation Service. I spent five years under their sponsorship and they took away a number of the most significant practical obstacles like transport. For five years they provided me with hire cars and Commonwealth cars to take me to and from school and university. The cost to them is little compared to the benefit that it brought to me in overcoming one of the major obstacles I had. So that sort of practical support was absolutely crucial.

I don't know that we've lost sight of it in the community at the moment, but we haven't understood the benefits that that apparent expenditure brings. I worked out a little while ago that I now pay as much in tax every quarter as the entire amount the Commonwealth Rehab. Service spent on me in five years. Now, just a straight economic argument says to me that is a very good investment for the community. In fact, most companies, for

ACCIDENT

example, would love to make that sort of investment and make that sort of return on investments. But the community hasn't understood that sort of thing.

The support from my family and particularly from my sister made the major difference. And expectations of the community are very important motivating factors ... driving factors too. I think my family had expectations—all of them did—my father, mother and sister. But particularly my sister, in a very subtle way. I don't think she ever put into words what she was really doing. I don't think she even understood what she was doing. But she came to see me every day I was in hospital for ten months—every day without fail. She was in 3rd Form at school then. I was sixteen and she was fourteen. But she came in during the week with her school books, and she'd just sit by the bed for a couple of hours and do her school work. And just be there. She'd give me a glass of water or she'd talk to me for a bit and whatever. But she was there. Apart from the fact that she was showing me that she loved me dearly—and you don't let down people who love you—she was basically saying that she expected I would continue with my life, and that she was there to support me in that. I don't think she even really consciously understood that's what she was doing. I don't think I understood it at the time either. It's only now that I look back on it. But that's what it did to me. I remember thinking, 'I can't let Jane down'. It was inconceivable that I would do that, that I would abuse this sort of love that she'd given me by not putting my best foot forward and overcoming it.

Apart from anything else, she loved me dearly and if she saw me not coping with my life it would have had a dreadful impact on her. On the other hand, if I made a success of it, it would be a good thing for her. So, while I don't think I ever really consciously understood that at the time, I know that's what was going on.

I know I put in extra efforts because of my family.

My mother was the same, she was a very determined person, and still is. She'd basically made it very clear that she would give me all the support that I ever needed; she would always be there. But when she did that she expected that I would put my best foot forward as well. And how on earth can you estimate the impact of that? It's just inestimable, really.

Was your parents' attitude that they wanted you to continue your life exactly as you'd planned it?
Yes, yes. And so did I. That was always my attitude.

Did you and your family ever put that into words?
Not really. I don't think I ever did and I don't think I ever have had any deep, emotional discussions with my parents about it at all. In fact, I'm not sure that I've had too many deep, emotional discussions with anyone apart from my wife. It's not that I'm reticent to do so, but I just never have. I don't quite understand that. Discussions were more at a practical sort of level.

What happened when you left hospital?
I went into hospital in April and I left in November. I then went for a short period of time to a Rehabilitation Centre. They basically said that I was there for assessment—I don't think that I was, but it was a bit of a holiday really. There was a bit of physiotherapy in the morning and I chased girls in the evening. But I was there for a couple of months and going back into school in February.

What was your rehabilitation program? How did you occupy your time?
Most days, I think, I did physiotherapy. I don't do any physiotherapy any more so I don't know why I did it all back then. It was good, though, to occupy a few hours. The physiotherapy included a bit of basic training to give

ACCIDENT

me as much manoeuvrability as I could manage, like rolling on my side and so on. I still haven't learnt to do most of these things. But some of it was a bit useful.

I did some occupational therapy as well. That was absolutely a total waste of time. I used to have very heated arguments with the occupational physiotherapists. They were absolutely intent on teaching me useless things, things that I knew were going to be of no value to me whatsoever. 'We will sew some loops on the end of your socks so you can get your socks on'—and every time they'd come up with these wacky ideas, I'd say to them, 'How quickly will I be able to get my socks on when I've perfected the technique? When I have learnt everything that there is to know about putting socks on, how quickly will I be able to do this?' And they would say with a very straight face, 'Well, you probably won't get down to much under half an hour but it's taking two hours now so that's a major achievement'.

And I'd say, 'Listen, when I get out of here I'll be going back to school and university and ultimately to work. I don't think I'm going to have half an hour to put my socks on every morning. So I'm not going to spend an inordinate number of hours now learning to do it, and you're not going to sew ugly black tags on the end of my socks when they're going to be of no value to me at all.' Oh! That was a wrong attitude! I'd have the professor come down from the hospital to tell me that my attitude wasn't right, that I'd never achieve anything with that sort of attitude. But I just stuck to the same argument. I said I would learn the things that I believed were going to be of value to me, that would be important things, like transferring in and out of a car. I knew I would be able to drive—not straight away because I didn't have enough strength earlier on—but I knew ultimately I would have enough strength. So, I'd be able to transfer into and out of a car. And I would need to do that if I was going to be as independent as possible. So I spent hours doing that because I knew there was going to be value in it. But putting my socks on taking half an hour! Do you take half an hour to put your socks on?

I told them, 'I will pay to have those things done which I know I can never do efficiently. And the things I know I can do efficiently, then I will put all my effort into doing those things.'

I think they finally understood. They could see I wasn't wasting my time. I didn't sit around and do nothing but I focused my time on the things that I thought were going to be of value. I spent a lot of time learning to type. I can't type particularly fast, about 60 words per minute, which is not breaking any speed records, but that's been an enormously valuable skill to me. As my colleagues, all the managers around IBM, sit there and go '#%&', I can actually perform that small task quicker than they can. So that's a principle that I've applied from the beginning. I recognised very early on that the sort of jobs I'm most efficient in are the ones that don't require any physical activity. I can talk OK and I can talk on the phone OK. I can make decisions. So, those are the things I use in my working life.

The most important reason why I've been able to move through the ranks at IBM is that my physical disability is just irrelevant to the job. The thing that still has a bit of an impact is travelling. I do a lot of travelling both interstate and overseas and that's still a challenge to me. It's tough getting from one city to another. The airlines are usually good—they are now quite experienced and provide assistance with luggage, lifting me into aircraft seats and so on. But other forms of transport, particularly taxis, are really difficult. They are bad in Australia but in most other countries they are worse. The Asian countries simply don't have wheelchair accessible transport of any kind.

And of course when I stay in hotels I always need help for personal care—getting in and out of bed, going to the

ACCIDENT

toilet, getting showered and dressed. I need to hire a nurse in the place I'm going to, or when I travel overseas to take someone with me. Fortunately IBM has been wonderful with this—they pay either a nurse or someone (usually my sister or one of my carers from home) to travel with me.

Access to buildings—offices and hotels—is always a challenge. In most countries I travel to, including the USA and Europe, facilities are appalling for people who use wheelchairs. The beds are too low, the bathrooms rarely ever have showers that can be accessed in a wheelchair, even small things like the door handles on most hotel doors are round knobs. More than once I've had to call reception to open the door to my room so I can get out.

One of the worst experiences I've had travelling was last year in India. I had to work in Bangalore, which can only be reached from Madras. I arrived at the hotel in Bangalore after staying overnight in Madras only to find that my wheelchair had collapsed—the frame had snapped from metal fatigue. The hotel had a wheelchair which had come out of the ark, and I couldn't use it. I asked the hotel manager to get my chair fixed at any cost overnight. He said his brother-in-law could fix it. He did but the metal in the chair is an alloy that requires special welding and the chair collapsed again the next day. I ended up having to cut the trip short.

Can you tell me about your experience returning to school after the accident?

I went back to school and did my HSC. I missed 5th Form altogether. When I was in hospital they actually set up one of those correspondence systems, but there were other things to do in hospital rather than correspondence schooling so I missed most of it . . . I did a little bit of work but not very much. By that stage, I'd had enough of hospitals anyway. I found when I got back to school it didn't make any difference because, the way the course had been structured, most of the subjects were new material in 6th Form anyway. So while I hadn't had, for example, the books in 5th Form for English, there were a new set of books in 6th Form. So it wasn't such a big deal. The only subject that I found I was really behind in was Maths because the curriculum was a two-year curriculum, so I ended up having a tutor in my last year of school to bring my speed up in Maths.

I did fine in the HSC. And in fact, the headmaster rang me up when the results were announced and said that I'd got the highest mark of any of the science students. He was most impressed and congratulated me on the result. But I didn't do super-brilliantly. I wouldn't have got into Medicine—not that I was going to be a particularly great brain surgeon. I don't think there are too many people lying on the operating table who would be encouraged by the idea of someone in a wheelchair coming in with a scalpel. And I abandoned the idea of doing engineering because back then, in particular, it was still very much a physical thing and you needed to draw using manual drawing techniques. These days it would probably be easy to do.

So I started an economics degree. And I think I chose all the wrong subjects at university. I failed three out of four subjects in the first year, and that was because I did absolutely no work whatsoever. I was just dreadful. In terms of study I had this inability to really focus on long-term, theoretical sort of things. And that hit me in spades during my first year at university. I was probably still coming to grips with the disability and all aspects of it, too. So I did absolutely no work. I don't think I ever opened a book. How I ever passed one subject was a major achievement! I picked up that one subject—psychology. I passed that. It was the only non-economic subject I did. Then I changed over to Arts the next year and was fine from then on. Towards the end I was doing really well. I went back and did economics and political economy.

ACCIDENT

Consequently I'm really interested in politics and may well use that interest one day, but back then I had no interest in it at all.

I took on standard economics, majored in psychology and got my degree in the end. Before I'd even had my results from university I saw this advertisement for marketing people at IBM and applied. The only thing I knew about the company at that stage was that when I was in hospital one of the occupational therapists suggested that I write to this company called IBM, because the typewriter that I was learning to type on was an IBM typewriter. So I wrote to somebody in IBM and said, 'Could you give me a typewriter?' and they did—I've still got it somewhere. But that was all I knew about them.

What did you know about marketing at that stage?

Nothing. In fact, I didn't know a thing about anything really. But I saw this ad and I thought, Well, they were good enough to give me a typewriter, they might be all right to work for. So I went to this interview. I went to a whole lot of other interviews as well but you probably haven't got enough space in your book for some of the stories about my early job interviews. They were quite amusing. I remember one interview in particular with a life insurance company for the job of trainee manager. The interview had gone fairly well until the interviewer said, 'One of the requirements of the job is that you spend time selling life insurance and that means door to door . . . how will you get into peoples' homes?' I knew I'd lost it when all I could come up with was, 'I'll sit outside the front gate and call out for the person to come to the gate.'

I'd always made a habit when I went to interviews of never letting them know in advance that I was in a chair because if I told them over the phone they'd say, 'Oh, well, really . . . it's not . . .'. I thought, I've got to get in front of these people first and talk them into it. So, I adopted that approach.

I turned up at this interview and the guy I met there was just wonderful. He was in IBM for years and years after that and when he retired I went to his retirement dinner. He was a very nice guy—one of the world's really good people. He interviewed me, they gave me an aptitude test and I did that well. He said to me, 'Well, I'm impressed with the way you come across and you've done well in the aptitude test. I'll organise another interview.' The next interview went very well and I was gaining more confidence. I was becoming more impressed with the people I was meeting too.

I remember the process: at first I had this initial interview with personnel and then I had single interviews with three marketing people because it was a marketing job I was going for. I knew the minute I walked into the third interview that I had the job. The guy's whole manner implied, 'I don't even know why you're here. Everybody else has said that you've got this job.' So he asked a few questions and said, 'As far as I'm concerned the job is yours'.

But I've learnt subsequently that it threw the whole place into a dilemma, they didn't know how to handle the situation at all. They went to head office and said, 'We've got this guy here who is a quadriplegic in a marketing job and we're going to expect him to go to see customers. How do we handle this?' Apparently head office came back and said, 'Well, you're on your own. We don't know how to handle this either.' The first guy I met who offered me the job—and I remember the interview very clearly—said, 'If you're willing to take the job we'd like to have you. There are just a couple of practical things. Firstly, you drive a car so you need parking. We'll make a commitment to you now that wherever you work in IBM we will always provide parking.' And they have done that all the way along the line. In the city you can imagine what the cost of a parking space was. In my job I'd get a parking space anyway these days but when I first started I was a lowly, bottom-of-the-rung trainee and

ACCIDENT

they gave me a highly valuable inner-city car-parking spot. There are a lot of companies around that still don't do that. In some government departments for example, it's still a fight to get parking.

They also said, 'We'll expect you to travel in your job. You've described to us how you would do that but what you've basically said is that you need someone to be with you. That's fine. We will always either send your wife or your partner with you or we will pay for a nurse.' And again, there have been absolutely no questions asked about that ever since. It's cost IBM a few dollars over the years, but I had a talk to our Managing Director a little while ago, informally, about this sort of thing and the message back was very clear. He said, 'When I look at the sort of responsibility you've had in IBM—my current business responsibility is worth about $138 million a year—why would we even question having a nurse help you for two hours a day at $13 an hour?'

I don't do it all alone, I've got a team of people working for me, but nevertheless he said, 'Why would we question it? It's just a nit . . . an absolute nit.'

What is your job?

I'm the International Marketing Manager for Australia and New Zealand and the Asia-Pacific Region. On a day-to-day basis, it's just like most other management jobs, and I find it really interesting. I love the job because it's an area that's not particularly well defined in IBM. IBM is a highly-structured company and there are ways of doing most things which have been developed over the years. But in this area it's really dealing with all of IBM's international customers, so all the large customers we have in Australia, like National Australia Bank, Department of Immigration, NSW TAB, actually operate all over the world in a whole lot of other countries, and my responsibility to them is to make sure that they can do business with IBM as easily in, let's say, Beirut as they do in Melbourne. The National

Australia Bank is a huge customer of IBM in Australia. You can imagine the sort of support they've got, people coming out of their ears and a huge team of people working on the account. But in Beirut . . . well, who's ever heard of National Australia Bank? So IBM Beirut is not particularly big, but the bank expects the same level of service from us there as they get here, quite rightly so. And it's my job to make sure they get it. Customers who have headquarters elsewhere but do business in Australia—like Citibank, Mercedes Benz, Toyota and so on—need focus because the technology they're installing here, while it's not worth an awful lot, needs to be integrated with their world-wide systems and I've got to make sure that they get the right level of support here.

In the end those international customers bring in about a quarter of IBM's worldwide business. It's only about 3000 customers who fit into that category out of literally millions of customers we have worldwide but they bring in a quarter of our revenue, so they're very important to us. It's my job to meet those customer requirements by providing global support, contracts, processes and so on. I also get involved in a whole range of other international issues. Any document or phonecall to IBM Australia or New Zealand which mentions the word international is automatically directed to me.

Do you travel a lot overseas and interstate?

Yes, but I don't do anywhere near as much interstate travel as I should. In fact, this year, since I took on the Asia-Pacific role, I've been travelling more overseas.

How big is your staff?

There are fourteen here in Australia, mostly in Sydney and Melbourne, two people in New Zealand and then one in each of the other Asia-Pacific countries, apart from Japan where there are four. In terms of management you can't effectively manage people in, say, Korea the same way you

ACCIDENT

manage people in Sydney. So in the end it's far more important to pick the right people who have the right experience where I can't really add any value to them, even if they were in the same office. Then I basically delegate the work, make them aware that I'm here and they just get on and do the job.

Outside IBM you've been very involved politically in working for people with disabilities. Tell me about that.

I'd have to say that the things I do outside IBM really give me a greater sense of achievement. Not that there's anything wrong with IBM, there's not, it's basically helped me get to where I am and given me all the skills that I use outside. But in the end, from the social point of view, what I'm doing at IBM is really helping IBM make a profit, which in the end helps shareholders. There's nothing wrong with that. I don't have any moral objections to that at all, but at a personal level I feel that if I get to the end of my productive life and think that all I did was to help IBM shareholders make more profit, then I will think that I have wasted my life.

So I use the skills I have gained at IBM to help, as much as I can, other organisations which haven't had the same exposure and experience. And it's surprised me just how valuable those skills are. In achieving an objective I think you apply the same business principles to any sort of organisation—whether it's the Australian Quadriplegic Association or the NSW Adult Community Education sector. Because I think those basic business principles are not just business principles, they're principles for getting people to work together for common goals to achieve something. And I really enjoy applying those skills that I've learnt in IBM to help these other organisations achieve their goals.

Over the years I've done quite a few different things. I was chairman of the board of the Australian Quadriplegic Association for about five years, and I've been on a group called The Australian Disability Consultative Council now for twelve months—that's a Federal Government advisory body which advises the Federal Government on disability issues with representatives from a whole range of disability areas as well as representatives of the various ministers involved. I'm actually representing the Employment Minister. And I enjoy that. I think I can bring something to that. I'm not an expert in disability because I haven't focused my entire life on disability, so I'm a little bit short on understanding all the issues that a whole range of people with disabilities face. But I can bring some business skills to the process and that seems to be valuable—basic things like defining what your objectives are. Articulating those into a vision. Communicating that vision to people so that they share in what you're trying to do. Identifying what tasks need to take place to achieve that vision and allocating those tasks and ensuring that people understand what their role is in achieving those things. Setting up measurement criteria so that people can understand if we're actually doing what we've set out to do. In the disability area it's no good saying, Well, we want to provide independent living options for people with disabilities. We need to know how many people with disabilities we are going to help. And how you are going to know that the million dollars you're spending on that is achieving the maximum outcomes for those people. Would you be better to spend the million dollars in another way? Is that going to give a better return? It's fairly basic stuff and there's no rocket science in it at all, but it's amazing how many of these groups haven't got a clue how to go about doing that. So, I can come into a group and help them manage the process.

And you do a lot of public speaking.

Yes, I suppose I do. But it's mainly in three areas. Whenever I get the opportunity to talk about disability and the things that we need to do to allow people with a disability to fulfil their potential and contribute, I take those opportunities. I also talk about adult and community education, and I talk about motivation generally.

I really enjoy doing it. Without being at all self-denigrating, it's one of the few skills that I have, really. I mean, I can't do many physical things but this is something that I can do. The disability has no impact whatsoever on my ability to talk to people—none. And when you think about any management job, that's all management is.

You mentioned earlier that you had been married. Would you like to talk about your marriage?

I was just twenty years old when Julie and I first met. We met at university in third year psychology—Julie was doing a degree in Social Work. I'd noticed her in lectures and tutorials; she was quite beautiful. I found her very attractive and I was attracted to her intellectually as well.

I remember the day we met I was on my way to a lecture, pushing down the road when Julie came up behind me and asked, 'Do you want a hand?' I said, 'Yes, please!' I would never have plucked up enough courage to ask her to go out, so at that moment the ice was broken. That day I asked her if she'd like to go to the theatre and afterwards I worked out the logistics of how we'd get there, thought it all through . . . my sister would get the tickets and so on. The next week when I saw her, she asked me if I'd already gotten the tickets and I asked her why. She said that on the night we'd arranged to go, she'd forgotten that she had a 21st birthday invitation. Now this was one of the critical moments in life. I had to make a split-second decision: I could either say no, I haven't got the tickets, that's fine, knowing that was the last time I would ever have asked her to go out with me; or say, as I did, that yes, I already had the tickets. So we went to the theatre. There was a terrific rapport between us and three months later we were engaged.

Julie's mother announced our engagement at my 21st

birthday party and it floored some of my family. I remember one of my aunts asked, 'Who is she marrying? Mark? Is Mark getting married?' They were floored! We were married six months later at Newington College, my old school. It was a very romantic affair.

We were married for sixteen years and from my perspective it was the most wonderful marriage. I think the biggest problem we had was that I always thought that the best thing about the relationship was that we shared a single life. And we did. We did everything together, had a lot in common, shared similar philosophies of life. Now I realise it was a life based on me. She took away all the impact of my disability. She worked a full-time job as well as looking after me, often getting up at five in the morning. She allowed me to lead a completely normal life but in doing so never had a life of her own. She needed a life eventually, and that is why quite recently we finally separated. I didn't ever mean to take advantage of her, or hurt her, I would never have done that consciously. But we shared 'my' life and I had interpreted that as sharing a single life. I now realise how much of an imposition it was on her.

The divorce has been the worst thing that has ever happened to me. Much worse than the disability. Two years down the track I'm still trying to cope with it. I loved her very much. I've been to see a counsellor several times since and she's pointed out that both parties are equally responsible in a marriage break-up, that Julie should have said something so that we could have tried to work things out earlier. But in this case, I don't believe that both parties had equal fault. Julie didn't say anything because she loved me and she wanted everything to be right for me.

Coming to grips with losing Julie has been terrible, and sorting out the practical problems of Homecare, organising my life, has made it the worst eighteen months of my life. But I'm surviving on all my own efforts now and not hurting anyone in the process.

My lifestyle has changed, my circumstances have changed a lot. I would have said two years ago, when Julie was still here, that my life was basically perfect. There was just nothing that I would have really changed about it at all. I was functioning in a good job. I was enjoying my social life. Nice home. I had everything, I was just enjoying life totally. But since Julie left, I realise that she was relieving one of the major impacts of the disability by being here and basically looking after me—doing all my personal care and so on.

Not only did she do that extremely well, because she was very competent and very caring, but she was with me all the time so there was never a time when I was exposed. If anything ever went wrong my wife was always around to fix it. We even worked together in the same company, in the same location so if anything happened at work and something went wrong, she'd be there. I understand now that there were a lot of negative aspects to that. But I never have the option of not needing that sort of support because I can't do things to help myself. I just physically can't do it and never will be able to do my personal care. So I'm always going to need that sort of support. But now I'm relying on an external service to do it, the Homecare service.

I've been struggling with the service for months and still I'm struggling with it to gain any real level of flexibility. When my wife was here, for example, I'd just say, 'Oh, look, I'm ready for bed'. Perhaps she'd say, 'I might stay up a little bit longer but if you're ready I'll put you to bed' . . . or whatever. That would be it. I mean, I just wouldn't think about it. It was just like leading a normal life. Just as you normally would if you were with a partner, you'd say, 'Are you coming to bed now?' In this case my wife had to actually do some work to make it happen. And I never realised the true impact of that, but it just made my life totally normal—I could do anything I wanted to at any time.

Now I find that even after months of constant struggle and discussions with Homecare about the need for me to have flexibility so that if I wanted to go out tonight to dinner, I could say I don't want to go to bed at 9.30, I want to go to bed at 10.00, or maybe even make a phonecall on a mobile phone to say, I'm ready to go to bed now, can you meet me at the house, I just can't do that. They're starting to make some changes to it after an awful lot of pressure, but it's been a constant battle to try to get them to understand that if I'm going to lead the sort of normal life that keeps me motivated, keeps me making a contribution and going to work, I need to have the flexibility to run my life along those sorts of lines.

I understand there are challenges that we'll need to work out together, and they will be worked out. Over time there have been significant changes they've made to provide some extra flexibility for me. But I can also see over these months just how demotivating that's been for me. It's been such a struggle and so demotivating to think, I can't go out with my work colleagues tonight because my Homecare person is scheduled to come at 9.30 and I know I can't change it. And my work colleagues might say, 'Oh, you can't come tonight? And the next morning, 'We had a great night last night, It's a shame you weren't there'. Well, in the end I get angry about that and I complain about it and try to get it changed. But I can see just how incredibly demotivating that must be for the majority of people who have a disability, who don't know the right people to talk to, don't know the right way to approach it, don't have the motivation to actually do something about it, to keep fighting the system all the time.

These things have got to be changed; these are the things that I think are most important, from a disability point of view, to change in the community. To try and remove those infrastructural barriers which are there so that people can generally, without a struggle, live a normal lifestyle. When those barriers are removed it means that people can go to work, pay taxes, make a real contribution and not have to take a pension or whatever. But we come back to the same thing, the community hasn't understood that there's an investment to be made in order for that to happen.

What are your other interests outside work? What about your love of music?

I've got a CD collection that I listen to. Listening to music would be one of my greatest pleasures. I've got a hi-fi system that's really lovely and I probably went a bit berserk with that but it was worth it. This sounds a bit ridiculous but I even like going shopping. I've started doing that since my wife left and I actually enjoy it. I like going around looking at all the things. I usually spend much more than I should because they have all these things sticking out in the aisles, and I look at them and think, Oh, yes, I wouldn't mind one of those.

I used to absolutely love boating. I got really quite obsessed with it, and that's one of the problems that created the situation where my marriage wasn't going to survive. I think the boat was probably my worst obsession. It was a 36-foot cruiser with two bedrooms, seven berths, kitchen, bathroom . . . it's gone now. When my wife left it got sold. Oh, I love the water. I can't even describe why. I just love it.

So if you haven't got your own boat now, can you perhaps hire one?

I can't really do that. Boats are the most inaccessible things on earth for me. I had to spend a fair bit of money in getting the boat set up. There's a thing that takes jet-skis on and off boats. It's like a crane. I had one of those fitted to the boat and a harness designed for the chair so that my wife could just press a button and the chair would go up and across and down. It was terrific, it really was wonderful but still heavy work for my wife. And in the end I really spent a lot of money on it. I just got obsessed with it, I think partly because I loved it so much but partly because this was something that I was going to make work.

With or without a boat, your life is very full and busy. How would you sum up your personal philosophy about what is important in your life?

I'd say my life is influenced by two things. Firstly I do have a philosophy, if you could call it that, that you only get two choices in life: you either make the most of what you've got (or haven't got) or you go under. People say to me all the time, 'I'd never be able to cope with what you cope with.' I say in reply, 'Well, I can either use the skills and talents I still have to create a fulfilling life (and I have) or I can do nothing and die unfulfilled'. Of course sometimes I don't feel like saying that, so I just say, 'Get lost!'

I could go deeper into my personal philosophy—that I don't believe in religion; that I feel I have a responsibility to society to use whatever strengths I have to make a difference to the world around me; that most people are inherently good (with some marked exceptions); that the simple things in life make it worthwhile; and that life is good . . . but it all sounds a bit disjointed.

The thing that influences me probably as much as my personal philosophy is that I was born an optimist. I don't like bad things to happen (and my life has had a few of them) but life is simply not all bad . . . there's always something to look forward to and I just can't let anything—my disability included—get in my way.

What all this means, of course, is that I've been lucky. I was born with a positive outlook on life, with a good mind and a high level of motivation. I've had great support, I've put a lot of effort in and I've more often than not been in the right place at the right time.

Not everyone is so lucky, of course. All these factors have meant I've been able to overcome many of the obstacles our society puts in my way—primarily an inaccessible environment and a narrow-minded outlook. But virtually by definition not everyone is going to have the same level of good fortune that I've had. While I think the community needs to lift its expectations of people with disabilities, it also needs to recognise that the massive infrastructural barriers which it puts in the way of people with disabilities is demotivating. The community needs to accept responsibility for removing those barriers so that people with disabilities can make the contribution to society that they can and want to make.

2

Janine Shepherd

A world-class cross-country skier, Janine was critically injured in a near-fatal road accident during the period leading up to the 1988 Winter Olympics in Calgary, where she was to compete.

When she greeted me at her home on the day we first met, there was an immediate rapport and I was moved by her immense warmth. Her spirited zest for living is contagious and I am richer for knowing her.

ACCIDENT

Janine, you were very athletic from an early age. Why was sport such a passion?

I was a very active child and my life revolved around being outdoors. I was never an indoor type of person. I guess I was a tomboy. I was a third daughter and in a sense the son that my father would have loved—not that he regretted having a daughter—but because of that, I was always the tomboy doing the rough-and-tumble things like riding skateboards.

I started my athletic career at the age of six with Little Athletics, when it was first starting in Australia and that was really an outlet for me. I became very involved in that and it became my life until I was at least thirteen. It took up my every waking moment: I trained during the week, ran every day, I competed on weekends, then later on I got into the senior ranks. I felt it was what I was born to do. I was an athlete and that's what I was good at. I was built for it as well: I was very lean, very strong and it all came so easily to me. Whatever I tried I picked up very easily, but I also worked hard at it. I never took it for granted, I trained extremely hard and I was obsessed by it—I loved it. I just loved to push my body and was fascinated by that feeling of trying to explore the limits of how good I could get at things. It was my life.

I started off as a sprinter and then I got into race walking, and I set an Australian record in that which still stands. Then I had a bit of a break around my teen years, maybe because I was going through those troubled times that most teenagers do, and I didn't want to be different. And I didn't want to be in a State team or a sporting team when all the other kids were having parties and good times, so I had a rest for a while, which I needed in order to work out what I really wanted. Eventually I got back into running and later on long-distance running.

I did this right through to my late teen years and then I went to university. By then I'd been skiing for quite a few years but I hadn't begun cross-country skiing. Prior to that I had played State netball and softball through school. I was involved in team sports for a long time. Then at university I got more into individual sports like triathlon which was really only starting to be popular then. I did very well at it and became the New South Wales Triathlon Champion. I guess a lot of people look back and think I should have stayed with triathlon because now it's quite lucrative and it will be an Olympic sport. But I had also started cross-country skiing, as all my friends had, and that became my obsession, my passion, and I just loved it. I was really built to ski. I had a very strong physique, very low fat percentage and a good relative muscle percentage. I also had an extremely high oxygen intake. I think you're born with a certain capacity in terms of oxygen intake, but I also know that because I'd trained and been an athlete all my life, it was something that had developed further. So I had the ideal physique and psychologically speaking I was perfectly prepared—I'd found the sport that was right for me in every way.

During winter we would race here in Australia and in our summer we raced in the European winter. Then when we were off snow we did a lot of long-distance endurance training, a great deal of long-distance running as well as sprints and hill training, work on roller-skis, and with new skating techniques including a lot of speed skating.

It's a very technical sport and it's also extremely demanding in terms of endurance. In fact, cross-country skiers have the highest oxygen intake of any athlete in any sport—more so than marathon runners, for example, because it's like running a marathon but on skis and at altitude, so it's extremely demanding.

I loved it because I'm a bit of a glutton for punishment, and I strive to push myself to the limit. I'd found this incredible sport that was to become my whole life. It was easy for me because I was so physically fit when I started doing it that it was just a matter of getting the technique right. The new technique of skating was ideal for Australians because it wasn't technically as demanding as the classical technique which really needs to be practised from birth if you want to compete against the Norwegians, for example. For me it was just perfect.

After the short time it took for me to pick it up, I really raced up through the ranks. I still had a long way to go in terms of catching up with the Europeans, but there was no doubt in my mind that I could get there because I could see the progress I was making in a short time, and I knew that for me it was just on-snow experience and also race time that I lacked. I needed to get over to Europe and train with the people who were the elite skiers at the time.

I was approached by the Canadian ski team and coach to join up with the Canadian team. He said, 'We really think you can make it, but it's going to be near impossible if you stay in Australia with the Australian team', because we were so small and we had nothing in the way of facilities.

It was really a fantastic opportunity for me and a great compliment to be invited to go and train with them. I jumped at the opportunity. I would still be an Australian, but I would be in their team, using all their facilities, training with their girls, being pulled along by them. I would be able to take advantage of their experience. It was all very exciting.

So for two years prior to the 1988 Winter Olympics in Calgary, I would have been with them. I was just on top of the world with this incredible opportunity. For my whole life I'd felt that I had been working towards something like this. I always felt that I'd go to the Olympics in some event. That was my goal in life.

I am very competitive, which I used to think was a bad thing. I occasionally thought I was becoming too competitive but now I don't think so. It depends on the point of view you take. I think that if you look at competition as pushing yourself to be the best that you can be, then it's a positive thing. I've always had a competitive streak—not because I want to be better than anyone else, but because I'm quite obsessed by how good I can become and realising my full potential. So if competition pushed me to be the best and pushed me towards uncovering my potential, I think that's a good thing.

What's behind that driving spirit, that competitive spirit? Not everyone has it.

Perhaps it's something that's developed when you start sport at a young age. There are many traits you pick up from sport which are so important. That's why I think it's essential for children to be involved in sport because so many of life's lessons are learnt by doing it. You learn to appreciate that nothing comes without hard work. You've got to try hard if you want to get ahead, and you learn to work as part of a team and to stand on your own two feet at the same time. You learn that you don't always win, but you've got to get in there and have a go anyway.

But to become one of the elite, to become a champion, does take something extra and that's not just physical power or an ability to endure pain, it's a particular psychology, wouldn't you say?

I can see that there is probably something there that makes me extend myself a little bit further than other people. Why is that? I think that basically some people are more motivated, are more enthusiastic than others. Obviously some are more competitive than others; but there are also people who are too competitive and it becomes unhealthy because a balance has to be found.

We all have a different make-up and I am very much the sort of person who, when deciding to do something, puts 110 per cent effort into it. I really want to excel, see

ACCIDENT

how high I can go, how far I can fly, and that's what keeps me going.

Were you able to compete as a skier while you were at university?

I was actually deferring my studies because Marty Hall—the Canadian coach—had said to me, 'If you want to do well you can't stay at university and ski; you have to choose'. So I was in the process of arranging that. I'd written away and deferred my studies at university for a couple of years to concentrate on skiing. I was making plans to go and train with the Canadian team in preparation for the '88 Winter Olympics.

My life revolved around my sport and all my friends were athletes, so a social event for us was going for a 20 km run together. We had a different lifestyle but it was great and we all had similar interests and goals. And we all had a very healthy lifestyle. But I suppose that in a sense it wasn't a totally balanced one because we were involved in sport and nothing else.

What were the events leading up to the near-fatal accident which changed your life?

I'd planned to go on a bike ride with my fellow team mates from the ski team and some other athletes. We were riding from Sydney to Katoomba, up in the Blue Mountains, which is about a four-hour bike ride. I had originally decided not to go because I was feeling quite tired and I thought I was anaemic. I had been training quite hard and thought I needed a rest, but a friend was coming up from Victoria and I decided, 'Oh, I can do it. I'll just do this ride and then I'll rest'.

One day prior to that I'd had a blood test to test for anaemia which is quite common in female athletes. But I'd decided I'd go on the bike ride, so that morning I kissed Mum goodbye, got on my bike, and my friend got on his bike and off we went. I called, 'See you tonight,

Mum, I'll be home for dinner', and I set off to meet up with the rest of the group of twenty or so. It was something we did a couple of times a year but it was also an LSD training—Long Slow Distance training. It's nice to be able to train with your friends, and so it becomes a social event as well. And it was a beautiful sunny day.

Once I got on my bike and started pedalling I was happy. It was a hot day—I remember I stopped and took off one of the jacket layers, packed it into my bum-bag, put that around my waist, then got back on my bike and was away again.

We met up with the rest of the group at Castle Hill and continued out through Kellyville. We stopped off a few times—we'd regroup and stop for ten minutes and have a drink and something to eat before setting off again. We did that all day. I guess we'd been on our bikes for about four hours when the accident happened.

With hindsight I'd say that I would never ever cycle up there again. It's terribly dangerous. When we got to the hills through the mountains I started feeling pretty weary because I had been over-training; I had been through quite a strenuous period, so I started to slow down.

I was the only woman in the pack. One of my close friends was just up ahead of me, and one was right behind. We'd gone up through the mountains and we were riding up Boddington Hill which is the hill that leads up to Katoomba. I remember passing a friend and having a few words to him as he was slowing down. I just pushed on and that was one of the last things that I remember.

It was about 3.30 in the afternoon, a gorgeous, bright day with clear blue skies. I remember I was up off the seat of my bike, riding with my head down, and my friend was about 100 yards behind. I had on a helmet, I was wearing a bright yellow shirt and all the right cycling gear that makes you easily visible on the roads. I don't remember

ACCIDENT

anything about the accident at all. That was it. That's my last memory, just cycling along up that hill.

I can tell you what other people have told me: As I was cycling along the side of the road I was hit by a speeding utility truck. At the time of the accident there was another car driving past. They looked up and saw something flying through the air and thought, 'What was that? Oh, my goodness, it's a body.' Of course, that was me when I was hit and I was catapulted way up through the air. I somersaulted and landed on my head.

Elizabeth, the woman in the car who saw me flying through the air, stopped and ran back. If it wasn't for her I wouldn't be walking today. She got there just as a couple of young guys were about to pick me up and throw me in the front of their ute to take me to hospital. If they had done that I never would have walked again. She screamed at them, told them to leave me alone, and then got blankets from somewhere to cover me up. Then she sat there with me, held my hand and talked to me. At that stage I think my helmet was gone—it had flown off with the impact and my head had been cut open. My skull was exposed, there was blood everywhere and I was foaming at the mouth.

Apparently I had my eyes open but obviously I couldn't see. I had that glazed look that you have when your eyes are open but you're unconscious. I was making an awful noise and trying to get up. And of course, I couldn't. Elizabeth said she tried to calm me. I was obviously in extreme shock. Another car had gone ahead and told my friend who rode back, so by that stage I had two of my friends from the group with me. There were people and cars everywhere and someone went off to call an ambulance. Elizabeth was saying to me, 'You're going to be all right. You're going to be all right. It's OK. Nevan is here . . .' Because she wanted me to know that I had friends with me. Finally the ambulance came, they put me on a spinal board and took me away. I think my friend

John went in the ambulance with me. Elizabeth thought that no one would ever see me again.

How fast was the utility travelling when it hit you?

He was going 80 km per hour . . . that's what he said he was going. I think he was actually going a lot faster than that. He said the sun was in his eyes but basically he was speeding. You know, if the sun is in your eyes and you can't see, you don't drive at 80 km per hour, you slow down, you pull over. You've got to see to be able to drive, and he just hit me. The seat was completely shorn off my bike; the metal looked as if it was cut with a saw, right through the middle piping. If you can imagine . . . I'm up off the seat of my bike, he's coming from behind and he just runs straight into me. So I must have gone way up. I took the brunt of the hit in my back and backside, so it ripped out all the flesh from my backside. I've got huge scars and you can see the flesh is gone. The impact sent me flying into the air, I somersaulted and landed on my head. Nobody thought I would live.

My neck and my back were broken in six places. My collarbone, right arm, five ribs on my left side, some bones in my feet were all broken. My whole right side was ripped open and filled with gravel. My head had been sliced open across the front exposing the skull underneath. I had internal injuries and I'd lost five litres of blood. So by the time the helicopter arrived at Prince Henry Hospital my blood pressure was 40/nothing. It didn't look really good.

Somehow the news filtered back home to my parents. I don't know how they were contacted. They were meeting their friends that night and Dad's best friend was a senior policeman so he thought he'd find out exactly what had happened because you often don't hear the real story. He rang the police in Katoomba and said, 'I'm Sergeant Elliott, what's happened to Janine Shepherd?' And they said, 'It's not good, she's not going to live.' So of course,

ACCIDENT

he heard this and thought, 'What on earth do I say to Max?'

When my friend John arrived at the hospital he phoned Mum and naturally didn't want them to panic, so he said, 'Janine has been in a bit of an accident, do you want to come up and get her?' So, they drove up to Katoomba thinking they were going to have to scold me. You know, 'Be more careful on your bike next time!', but not knowing at all how bad it was and how serious my injuries were.

There was a visiting doctor from England who had just arrived in Australia, at this lovely, quiet, little Katoomba Base Hospital and, of course, I arrived and they'd never seen such a mess. I had so many injuries. They knew that I had spinal injury because I couldn't move my legs. I was unconscious and didn't know what was going on.

Mum and Dad arrived at the hospital and went into instant shock. Mum said all they could see were my feet and a crowd of doctors. It's quite strange looking back on it now. Someone was looking after Mum and Dad trying to calm them down. All this action was going on in a little intensive care room up in the Katoomba Base Hospital and Mum heard one of the team say, 'I think we've lost her'. They asked Mum if she needed a sedative but she said, 'No, I can't. I need to know what's going on.' So at that stage they didn't think I was going to live.

They couldn't move me because I was losing a lot of blood . . . I lost five litres of blood which was probably all I've got. They were pumping it in and I was losing it all. They wanted to transfer me to a bigger hospital but they couldn't because of the blood loss. Then they rang the helicopter, describing it as a VIP emergency—apparently that's done so that the media can be alerted to an accident involving anyone the public will want to hear about. The helicopter brought some blood up so they were able to transfer me.

It was about 8 o'clock at night when the helicopter

arrived to transfer me to the hospital in Sydney. It was very cold—I think that must have been the feeling of cold that I remember, the only memory I have. I've tried to recall other details but it's not possible. Since that night I've become very good friends with the helicopter crewman and he told me, 'We didn't think you were going to make the helicopter flight, we thought we were going to lose you on the way because of the blood loss'. The blood loss was the big thing, not the broken bones.

Mum and Dad got in the car with Chris, my friend who had been with them all the while at the hospital, to drive down to Sydney thinking they were never going to see me again. Chris said that the drive down to Westmead Hospital was silent. Nobody spoke; the three of them were in shock.

They arrived at Westmead and nobody knew anything about me there. Someone finally told them that I'd been taken straight to Prince Henry Hospital. So they got back in the car and found their way to Little Bay which is on the other side of Sydney. It was getting late by then and it had taken them hours and hours, all the while not knowing whether I was dead or alive. It must have been horrific. I can only understand that now I have children of my own. I really feel for them now and what they went through.

Mum said the doctors didn't tell them anything because they didn't think I'd live. And then some time that night they let them in to see me. Mum and Dad slept at the hospital every night and they didn't go home for a week.

It was five days before they could say that I would live. On that first night some time in the middle of the night, the staff had told them, 'We've got accommodation for you, go and lie down, you have to leave. Just go and lie down or you're going to be wrecks.' Mum said she couldn't sleep anyway, she was just lying on the bed. And then early in the morning she heard someone calling, 'Mr Shepherd, Mr Shepherd, are you there?' And she thought, 'That's it, she's dead, they have come to tell us'. She

ACCIDENT

opened the door and the nurse said, 'It's OK, she's calling for you. Can you come up.'

Apparently I'd been calling out in the night for them. They came back to my bedside and stayed with me then. A couple of days later Dad went home to get some clothes because all they had was what they had been wearing when they drove to the hospital initially. I'd taken a turn for the worse and while he was at home the doctor called Mum outside and said, 'It's not looking good. We just don't think she's going to make it.' Unfortunately, Mum was alone so it was an awful lot to cope with.

By this stage I was having my own little experience. I guess I had what I'd call a near-death experience. There weren't any bright lights or white tunnels, but I had a strange experience where I was sweating and struggling and everything on one side was light and on the other everything was all dark. I could see what I'd call apparitions. There were these dark, horrible figures who were pulling me towards them. And I really think that that was a symbol of death.

I knew I was dying. I was being drawn and it was almost as if they were saying, 'Come with us and you won't have to be in pain', because I was in so much pain it was intolerable. I'd taken the brunt of the accident on my torso which was bruised black all over. At Katoomba they had stitched my head at the front and by that stage I had a plaster cast on my arm and there were tubes everywhere. They couldn't give me too many painkillers because of the head injuries, so the temptation to let go was strong. I remember feeling at one stage, 'I can't take this any more.'

That was the struggle, even though I was unaware of what was going on around me. I do remember clearly though, my father, his voice. He was stroking my head and squeezing my hand, that's all I remember, just his presence. It was so strong. He's a big man with these really big hands and this grip . . . it was just enough to keep me there, just holding me. And you know, at some time it was just like the dark went and the room lit up. And that was really the turning point between life and death. That's when the blood loss stopped—it just stopped, and that was it.

How long were you in hospital?

Almost six months. After surgery for spinal fusion they thought there was a chance I'd walk but with callipers and a walking frame. I'd have to use a catheter for the rest of my life. I'd have an 80 per cent loss of sensation from the waist down. I had one doctor say, 'Janine, you're never going to be able to do the things you did before, so you might as well accept that now', which was probably the best thing anyone could have said to me actually.

How long did you spend in a wheelchair?

Until I learnt to walk, really. But I rarely sat in the wheelchair, I always pushed it around. They used to say, 'Janine, you've got to get in the chair'. And I used to say, 'Look, how am I going to learn to walk if I get in the chair?' So I was this little frail figure of a thing and I used to push my wheelchair around the hospital . . . it probably looked very silly because there was no one in the chair. But I thought right from the word go, 'I'm going to beat this thing'.

You've described yourself as a very determined person, someone who is very involved in life. How much do you think your determination, that zest for living, contributed to pulling you through that barrier?

I don't know because it was such a subconscious experience. It wasn't as if I knew what was going on. I didn't think clearly. I honestly think that it was the power of love. I think it was my father and my mother who kept me alive. It was as if they were holding onto me. And if they hadn't been there things may have been different. I

ACCIDENT

have a very clear memory of this. It was like a warmth almost, and a light, just from Dad holding my hand. That's why I was calling for them, I needed them to fight for me. I think it was a battle we all fought. And I believe that was a really important part of it. There is a lot of healing that comes from the power of love, the people who support and love you.

What is your theory about recovery? Having sustained incredible injuries, why do you think you've recovered so well?

I think recovery is a very personal thing, and it's different for everybody. I think that my recovery has been 90 per cent mental and 10 per cent physical. I think the physical side is something that you deal with. People have to remember that it's all up here, in your mind—that's where it all happens. I probably worked that out pretty early and dealt with a lot of issues from the beginning, like knowing that I was going to have problems, so getting onto that quickly and not denying it.

Do you mean talking to people about it?

Yes. In the family, we talked and talked and we lived in it. It was very close. We got to the point where it was of no use talking any more because I wasn't getting any better. I needed to talk to someone who wasn't so close so I had some sessions with a psychologist because I had some huge issues to deal with. I was no longer an athlete. This had been my gift. Having it taken away made how much I'd lost so much clearer.

I had lost everything as far as I was concerned. I'd lost my sporting life, my career. Everything I had worked for all my life was gone. Talking with a psychologist helped to an extent but, in the end, I think that you've got to take charge of your recovery. No one is going to do it for you. You've got to do it for yourself.

I wrote to the guy who hit me. I wanted to have contact with him. And I took charge of the medical side.

I wasn't going to sit there and have people tell me, 'This is what you're going to do'. I said, 'Well, I'm going to learn about it. I want to know exactly what's happening to my body and the best ways that perhaps I can cope with it.'

I took charge in the sense that I knew a lot about my body because I was an athlete and, because I was in my final year of Physical Education teaching, I knew about the physiology of my body, I understood it better than anyone else could. I could better control my recovery. It was my body and I wasn't going to let anyone control it.

I was sick of the accident, the idea of this accident controlling every aspect of my life. I got to the point where I said, 'No. Blow you. You're not going to take my life away. I'm going to fight this. I'm going to get my life back. I want my life back.' I began to tell the doctors how I wanted to do things and what I thought about the way they did things. I was very determined and stubborn.

A big factor for me physically was that, having been an athlete with a strong and powerful body, I was now left with what I saw as a pathetic body. I had lost three stone in weight so I was incredibly frail. I was a bag of bones. I couldn't walk. I was in a wheelchair. But I suppose the worst thing of all was the internal injuries, the loss of dignity I experienced, partly because I now had to use a catheter. I had to deal with these things and they were huge issues. I was, or I should say am, a partial paraplegic. I had a body that had been in fine form before the accident. Learning to walk is one thing, but not being able to go to the bathroom when you want to took a lot of adjustment. It took away my sense of being a woman. I felt unclean . . . it was horrible. That was a big issue. I wanted to almost withdraw, and I wanted to run away. I felt it was unfair.

There were times when I didn't want to live. I didn't want to have to go through it all. But I fought it. I said, 'Damn. I have a right to live. I have a right to lead a

ACCIDENT

happy life. I have a right to be able to do things despite this.' So I took control.

Despite your fighting spirit and determination, did you grieve over what had happened to you?

Oh, horribly. When I got home from hospital and all my friends went away skiing and I was left at home, unable to walk, with a less than perfect functioning body, it was a real challenge. I was ashamed of my body. The frustration was unbelievable. I was an athlete, that was my whole life. I guess if I'd been a talented musician and I still had the use of my hands, that would have been a way to relieve the frustration, I could have sat there and belted out a tune on the piano or the flute or something. But I couldn't use my body. I couldn't put my shoes on and run out the door. There was nothing I could do. Nothing. The frustration was immense.

Did you feel anger too?

All that. Just crying, not wanting to get out of bed. I talked a lot in hospital and I'd gone through all the questions of Why? and God, why is this happening? I'd never had a strong faith before but suddenly the thought that it had happened for no reason, the thought that I was the brunt of some cruel joke, that there was a randomness about it, just BANG, that's it. Sorry, wrong place, wrong time, it's the end of your life. That didn't make sense.

I had to feel that there was a reason. That something had to come out of it. And that was really important for me. It kept me going, because deep down I thought, 'It's going to get better and one day I'm going to understand. One day I'm going to understand all this.' That was really important. It gave me a purpose, a reason to keep going.

Were you ever unrealistic? Did you feel that you would resume your former life?

Oh yes, I tried. I tried getting back on roller-skis and I kept falling over. I got all black and bruised. I had black eyes and cut lips trying to balance on snow skis. I tried hard to do that. I pushed myself incredibly hard. I think that is part of the reason I have recovered physically as well as I have.

People had said to me, 'The sooner you start exercising after an accident, the more chance you've got of a higher level of recovery because it's all to do with stimulating the nerves.' I don't know how true that is.

Many people are very seriously injured in terrible accidents. Given that all the factors are the same, the same age, level of fitness and good health, the same medical intervention, why do you think it is that some people, but not all, recover so well?

Well, this is just my personal opinion but I think there are a lot of factors involved. There is the degree of support you get from your family and friends. I had incredible support from my family and my friends who were all there fighting for me. It really helps to have those people there to help and love you and just be there. That was a big factor. My family and friends were with me all the time.

In fact, eventually it was exhausting because I had so many people there and I always felt I had to talk . . . but I wouldn't have had it any other way. I would rather that than not to have anyone there at all. But when it comes down to it, I think it's that fighting spirit, that will to live; it comes down to a certain attitude to life, a certain belief that life is worthwhile, that the fight is worth fighting for, that life is really worth it. It's a great world to be in no matter what happens.

The spirit that makes you want to fight back and reclaim some sort of life is the difference between being an optimist and a pessimist. An optimist will say, 'Oh,

ACCIDENT

well, there's got to be something I can do. I might not be the same any more but I'm going to go out there and overcome these obstacles.' Whereas a pessimist will say, 'It's no use, because things are never going to get any better and this is it'. So I think it all comes down to attitude. But I think it's possible to change your attitude. I think there are a lot of things that influence a person's outlook. It can be the people you mix with, the books and newspapers you read, the movies you watch, many things.

But you believe a positive attitude can be learned, it's not something that you're necessarily born with.

Yes, I believe that it's possible to learn a positive attitude and to change one's approach to life. To decide, 'Well, this is it. I'm going to start making a conscious effort to—it sounds a cliché—but look on the bright side of life.'

I am the sort of person who reads a lot of positive books and personal development books but I make a point of that because I see life as a big course in personal development. I think that people who make an effort and are positive are those who get ahead, see the good things. Those who constantly complain see everything as an obstacle and refuse to change.

The adjustments you've had to make in your life have been enormous, haven't they?

Very much so and it was tough. I became a person who was really ashamed of myself for a long time. I was ashamed of my body. I was ashamed of the fact that I had this less than normal body which didn't function like it was meant to function. That hurt for a long time because my self-image was shattered. I saw myself—this strong person, this in-control, assertive person with this very strong capable body—become a person who couldn't walk, at one stage, and then couldn't walk without help and then someone who would always have a limp. Someone who couldn't run and couldn't do certain things for herself for a long time. It took a long time to adjust to that.

But now I see myself as a powerful person because I choose to see myself that way. I discovered that the power isn't a physical power any more. The power is emotional and mental, and that's the difference.

I've learnt to use my mind to create the person that I want to be—a person who can do anything they want to do. I've learnt coping strategies. I still have bad days, I still have times when I look back and think, 'Gee, I wish I could do that. I'd love to put on my shoes and go out for a hard run.' I might be driving along and see someone jogging and I think, 'Gee, I wish . . .'. But I don't think that's unhealthy, it's not as if I sit and dwell on it. I can cope with that now. I know that I have certain means that enable me to handle that. It was different when I first had the accident, but I learned that through determination and goal setting anything is possible.

I decided that I was going to learn to fly an aeroplane—that was a big part of my recovery. I decided very early on that if I couldn't walk I'd have to find something else in my life and that's when I decided I'd learn to fly, which seemed ridiculous to everybody, particularly Mum. Hadn't she been through enough?

It was a huge thing to learn to fly at that point, because I knew nothing about aeroplanes. I had to ring up a school, I had to go out there and be with people I thought wouldn't like me or understand me.

How long after the accident was this?

It was about three months after I got home.

So about nine months after the accident, you were taking your first flying lesson.

Yes. I had to be lifted into the aeroplane. I was in a plaster body cast when I went for my first flying lesson. I had to wear the cast for three months and then a brace for

ACCIDENT

another three months so, I was covered in this big plaster slab. I had bones sticking out. I waddled like a duck.

I couldn't walk unless somebody was holding me up and I turned up at the flying school and said, 'Hi. I'm here for a flying lesson.' I looked ridiculous. They lifted me up into the aeroplane. I couldn't use my legs but I could use my arms and that was it. I said, 'I am doing this. I've got to do this.' And I knew I had to do it. That was my lifeline then to recovery. I had to do something that was almost ridiculous, something that other people couldn't do. I had to do something that was better than just driving a car. I had to do something that was almost out of reach. In a sense, flying was symbolic of my recovery.

And I guess everybody thought, 'She'll never do it. It's ridiculous.' Particularly, so early on when I was still recovering emotionally, to do something that was so radically different from what I'd done before.

I knew nobody in aviation so I had to put myself out there with all these people who didn't know Janine Shepherd, didn't know who I was as an athlete—just this strange girl who couldn't walk properly. When I look back on it I think, 'How did I ever do it?' But I did because there was nothing else. And it was little step by little step. The first thing I had to do was pass the medical. I didn't even think past there. I got past the medical and that was a whole story in itself, but I pushed myself. I pushed myself because I had set myself the goal of passing that medical.

Did you have to talk your way around some of that?

Oh, definitely. I told a few great lies to get through that. I just kept thinking, 'I'm going to do this. I'm going to do this.' I really wasn't thinking too far ahead, it was just, 'I can do this!'

So there I was studying aviation. It kept my mind active. It gave me something to look forward to. I loved it, the sense of freedom, being up in an aeroplane. And when I'd see my friends, there I was—this person who couldn't do what she'd done in the past but that didn't matter any more because I could fly an aeroplane. It was great for my self-esteem which had taken a real dive. So, for me, internally I guess I was saying, 'I can do this wonderful thing'. And life got better and better.

I then went on and got numerous other licences after that. I got my instrument rating, my twin-engine rating, instructor rating, commercial pilot's licence and my aerobatics rating. And then I became an aerobatics flying instructor . . . teaching people to fly upside down which was a bit of a shock to Mum and Dad who have yet to come up with me. Mind you, this all took a very long time and lots of hard work.

When I went back to university, I couldn't manage to finish the degree that I had begun, which was a Bachelor in Physical Education, but I was very fortunate that my lecturers at university were very understanding. They moved a few things around and I ended up a Bachelor of Human Movement Studies, which is a bit ironic, and then I went on and did a Dip. Ed. in PE and became a qualified PE teacher.

Even though I don't want to teach I felt that it was really important to finish my degree. A lot of people said, 'Why do you want to finish it? You've done all these other things, you don't need to do that, and you're not going to teach anyway', but something inside said, 'No, I have to finish it. I have to go back and do it'. I'd done all that university study and had nothing to show for it.

It was hard going back into that university mould and there was a lot of pain and memories in that all my friends, all my peers, had long since graduated. I felt in a way that I was starting again and it was hard getting motivated, to be in the right frame of mind, but I did. I'm now a university graduate and I very proudly hang

ACCIDENT

my degrees. And that is as much of an achievement to me as anything else I've done.

In the early days did you think that marriage and children were out of the question?

Definitely. Doctors didn't think I'd have children. But when they say, 'You're never going to do something', I have to go and do it anyway. And the recovery has been such a multifaceted thing. Having a goal to me is one of the most important things. Getting back into circulation, seeing friends again. And that's what I did. I challenged myself in a big big way. I did something which was the ultimate challenge. I got back into circulation and that was a huge challenge because I was dealing with some very big emotional issues about my body.

When I began to fly, my self image was protected because when I was in the aeroplane people couldn't tell there was anything wrong—that was important. I was making new friends. And I was putting myself on the line because why would anyone want to be friends with me, someone who was physically imperfect? I wasn't the athlete who could do everything now. I couldn't even drive. I had to get driven out to the airport all the time. So flying was a really big factor in having something to do. Writing the book was a huge part of the recovery too.

You've written *Never Tell Me Never* which has been an inspiration for a lot of people.

It's been incredible. I get letters from people saying that it has changed their lives. I feel very humble about that. The purpose of what has come out of all this has been helping other people realise that life doesn't have to stop after an accident. OK, it might never be the same, but it doesn't have to be of a lesser quality. It's just going to be different. And the letters I get aren't just from people who have had accidents, they're from people who have forgotten their dreams. It's helped them to realise that they should go out and do those things they've always wanted to do because they might not get another chance. Writing the book has been a very cathartic experience.

And then, being married. Emotionally I put myself on the line there again because I had to share my inner secrets with another person—a man. I felt I wasn't able to commit myself because I had things that I didn't want to tell other people. But suddenly I met this wonderful person who didn't care about those things and I realised they weren't important.

Did you meet your husband through flying?

Yes, Tim is a pilot. Tim is the sort of person I could ask, 'Would you rather I was normal?' and he'd say, 'Normal? How boring.' So that's been a great experience for me. And of course, having children, because I didn't think I'd have children. Suddenly, I've grown again. I've had two babies. I realise that I've gone one step further in the sense that my injuries just don't matter any more because I've got something more important than me, another life, another human life that I can put all my energies into and help grow and nourish. Often with injuries you tend to become self indulgent and you like to dwell on them. So having my two wonderful girls has helped me to see beyond that. Having them has helped me to understand that there are other things so much more important.

The medical profession really didn't think it was possible for me to have children and they said to me, 'If you do fall pregnant it will be extremely difficult, you probably won't be able to have a normal birth, you'll be in hospital for months and have to wear a back brace.'

So when I first fell pregnant I felt I was behind the eight-ball to start, but I took a very positive attitude, kept really fit, put on the minimum amount of weight and kept as active as I could swimming and doing weights. Towards the end of my pregnancy it became quite hard, because of the problems with my back, but in the end I had a very good pregnancy and a very normal labour.

Because of the fusion in my back, the pain was incredible as there was no flexibility when the baby was coming down. They also didn't think I'd be able to push the baby out, because I don't have normal pelvic tone, but I had known of at least one paraplegic woman who had had a vaginal birth, so I thought, 'If she can do it so can I, and I did it'. I had a very normal birth with Annabel. Charlotte was a little bit different because I had quite a few problems and a twenty-seven-hour labour. But I've had two births without any pain relief—not because I wanted to be a martyr, but because it was contraindicated. I can't have an epidural because of my spinal injuries.

So your life is a very full one, Janine. You're certainly as busy as most and more committed than many.

Yes I am. And you know, this whole experience has almost been like reading a really good book—you get to the end and suddenly the whole plot falls into place. You think, 'Oh, that's what it all meant. Yes, now I can see why . . .' You know, like those books that you just don't understand until you get to the very end.

Looking back now I can see why it's happened. I can see that if I'd gone to the Olympics that would have been great. A few people might have thought, 'Oh, good on her', but that would have died a natural death. Now so many more people are being helped by my accident and that's really encouraging for me. I wrote the book thinking, 'Maybe this will help someone going through a similar thing', and the old ideal of, 'If it helps just one, well great'. But it's encouraged so many more people and I've been helped by that. That has been my reward.

I think what it comes down to is that when we have accidents or trauma, or when people survive those awful massacres, those shootings, they help each other, they band together and they support each other. There's a great sense of love and a sense of unity. I think we have to remember that if we have an accident, we're not alone. Other people are out there going through it right now and we need to reach out to each other. That's really important in recovery—to feel that you're not isolated, to get back into the community again and back into circulation.

I've met so many fantastic people since the accident, people who have suffered and who are working hard to recover. That's been great for me.

3

Allana Arnot

It was a hot summer's day when Allana, a trainee pilot, was called out on a search-and-rescue mission to locate a crashed light aircraft. But the plane on which she was an observer also crashed, leaving her with dreadful injuries.

I watched her from a distance as she emerged from her car on the day we first met, walking-sticks steadying her as she came towards me down the hill to her house. I was conscious of her beauty and the smiling eyes which so clearly express her courage and determination.

ALLANA ARNOT

I was brought up in a very loving family and the youngest of three children. When I left school I worked as a Legal Secretary—nothing special at all. But it was a happy family life. Fairly uneventful, I suppose. I remember my brother, sister and I got together for Mum's fiftieth birthday and gave her a hot-air balloon flight as a present. The day she was supposed to go, she woke me up at four in the morning and said, 'Come on, come with me. I want you to come with me'. And so off I went down to Camden at four in the morning. I'd never done anything like this before. I was eighteen. I thought this is something different! So, off we went.

The balloon crew were there. A young guy named Laurie, who was a commercial pilot, was also a parachutist, and he worked with hot-air balloons. The pilot's name was Jim Murray and we all got on really well. I was just there to watch Mum, but I got involved in putting the balloon together and had the best time. I was hooked right there and then!

That morning—and my mum relives this often—my whole life changed completely. Within a week I'd broken up with my boyfriend, I'd left my job, taken up flying and I'd done a parachute jump. From that one morning I became a different person and I've never looked back.

I started working for Balloon Aloft which is what the company used to be called. About three weekends later I was helping to run a balloon festival for the Canberra Festival. I went on balloon trips, around Australia with the GIO Balloon, we used to go on tours and I worked on a thermal airship for a while. I started jumping out of aeroplanes. I started learning to fly . . .

That's how I met my husband Nigel. I was ballooning one morning and he came out to see the balloons. He had an old Tiger Moth—an old biplane—and he started doing joy flights, flying people around the balloon. We used to help each other. I'd encourage people to have a Tiger Moth joy-flight and he'd encourage his passengers to come

ACCIDENT

on balloon flights. We got on really well and started doing flying trips away together because I was learning to fly. And, inevitably, we fell in love. So, that's how it all began, my life of flying and meeting the man I love.

Our wedding day was beautiful. We were married in a small sandstone church in Cobbitty, not far from Camden airport. It rained a little but that didn't matter a bit, in fact, they say it brings good luck. Two of our friends surprised us with a Tiger Moth fly-past while guests were gathering in the gardens for the reception. The whole day was perfect. A friend took candid photographs and another friend made a great video which is now so precious to me because it's the only video I have of my walking before the accident.

The story of the accident begins when we received a phone call saying that an aircraft was missing—it had gone out on a training flight and hadn't come back.

Search and Rescue contacted Wing Commander Alan Hannah. He was an air-force pilot, an F–18 pilot, in fact. He was on leave and spending Christmas with us. So they contacted our home knowing that Alan was there. They wanted him to organise the search and rescue.

That was late on the afternoon of the 21st of December 1990. Alan went to Camden airport that evening to get things prepared for the next day. The search and rescue was to start at first light. As local pilots, we were also asked to take part in the search and rescue as people who knew the area and they allocated people to various aircraft for the search.

Nigel ended up going to work at the hangar and I was to go on a flight as an observer. We left at about eleven o'clock in a six-seater aircraft, so there was myself and five other people. There were two girls: me and another girl called Janine, who I hadn't met before, but I'd seen her a couple of times around the airfield. And there was Peter Whitehurst who was a very good friend. He was actually pilot in command. Then there was Alan Hannah who was living with us. There was another man sitting next to me whom I hadn't met before. And there was Robert Holmes who was a local pilot from Camden Airport whom I'd met a couple of times. So there were six of us.

We were given our area to search and basically briefed on what to look for—anything reflecting in the distance or anything that might be wreckage. We went up and started to zig-zag our search area, it was probably 40 or 50 minutes into the flight and we were over trees in the Burragorang Valley which is a very very rough area.

Suddenly there was a really loud bang. It sounded like metal going through metal and it was deafeningly loud. The aircraft started to shake violently and there was black oil spraying up on the windscreen.

It was obvious that there was a major problem. We really didn't have any choice but to land in trees. We couldn't get over the escarpment where there were clearer paddocks to land because we were too low and too far away. There was the dam, we could have landed in the water, but the pilot opted to go down the valley and to land in the top of the trees.

We were supposed to be going out Christmas shopping that day and I was having very odd thoughts that were irrational at the time. I was thinking, 'I should be doing my shopping, I can't be doing this.' There was no panic. No panic at all.

I had the two most qualified pilots I knew in the front seat and trusted them. I thought this landing was going to be more an inconvenience than anything else. I knew that we were in trouble but didn't think what was ahead. I had no concept of what was ahead. And it was only two-and-a-half minutes until impact.

There were probably a few bad decisions made in that forced landing situation. We could have been going a lot slower. We were flying down-wind instead of up-wind, so we could have been going a lot slower. There were also

ACCIDENT

other areas more suitable to land. However, about two-and-a-half minutes after the engine failure, we were at tree-top level and I remember hearing the wings hitting the trees. I felt as if I was in a washing machine, tumbling. I don't think we cartwheeled but that's the sensation I had. Tumbling. It was really noisy. I can remember it was very noisy and we were being thrown around. Then it just stopped. There was silence.

The first thing that I saw was a completely intact brain sitting on my lap.

A brain?

A brain. It was like a plastic model you might see in a doctor's surgery. And it was just sitting there. I thought, 'Oh my God, my brain's fallen out and it's on my lap!'.

And I started screaming and screaming. I remember what I was screaming because I just said it over and over again. I just kept screaming, 'Nigel, I'm dead! Nigel I'm dead!' And then I thought, 'How on earth can I be seeing this if I haven't got a brain? I wouldn't be able to see'. I was terribly confused. Then I looked up and I saw the top of Alan's head was missing from about . . . it was like an egg. The top of his head had been taken off. My first instinct was to push the brain off my lap and it fell on the floor.

And I remember there was so much blood everywhere. . . . Robert and Janine didn't die straight away so they were both alive for about ten or fifteen minutes. And semi-conscious. Janine never regained consciousness. After about ten minutes she just took a big sigh and that was it . . . she died. And Robert . . . every time he breathed he made this terrible gurgling sound. He finally drowned in his own blood. He started vomiting and that was it. He died. Steven, who was sitting next to me, was unconscious for about, I'd say, five or ten minutes. That was so strange because I thought he was dead. And when he regained consciousness it was such a shock.

After about ten to fifteen minutes. I could hear helicopters getting closer. It was a really hot day, it was so hot. And there was no wind whatsoever. I was in shock. I remember the heat and I remember the smell . . .

And were you conscious of your own injuries at this stage?
Yes. The first thing I did was to try to sit up.

I was in the seat and I was crouched over. I was half-leaning on Steven and I put my hand up on the chair, sort of supporting myself. I felt really short. I felt as if my head was close to my lap. What actually happened was that I'd sustained two impacts. The first one was when we hit the tree, that broke my back and threw me forward, so it stretched me. And it literally ripped the nerve endings out of my spinal column. The second impact, when we crashed, actually pushed me downwards. So I was about an inch-and-a-half shorter than I normally am.

I put my hand down my back and I could feel my spine sticking out of the skin, but it was a big lump. And I felt it grinding. So I knew that my back was broken. But, it's strange, my head was so clear. I was touching my legs and thought, 'I can feel my legs! That's fine.'

Then I saw the first rescuer pushing his way through the trees coming towards me. The shocked look on his face was what I remember about him. He broke the back windscreen to give us some air and to try to get to us. Then another person came. After about an hour all the television channels were there. Care-Flight, Westpac, Child-Flight, the police helicopter all arrived. There were a lot of helicopters on the ground and a lot of people. But they didn't try to get any of us out until the rescue crews got there, which was probably about forty minutes later. They got Alan and Peter out first and then Janine and Robert.

I remember them lifting up my right leg and saying, 'We're just going to straighten this out'. I looked down and saw that my foot was facing the other way. And when they straightened it, I didn't feel it. I didn't feel it at all. So I knew that I was in a bit of trouble.

Were you in pain at this stage?

Oh, terrible pain. Terrible pain. I sustained most of the impact in my stomach with the lap belt. I didn't have a proper seat belt so it was all taken in my stomach. It was so painful that I thought the seat belt had cut through my stomach. And because there was so much blood and flesh and bits of body parts all over me, I thought it was coming out of me. I felt that my stomach had been cut open. And in my back the pain was unbearable. It was terrible.

It took about three-and-a-half hours to get us out of the plane. I arrived at the hospital four-and-a-half hours after the crash. When they were taking me out of the plane, they took the seat out from in front because they had to sit me up. I knew it was going to be terrible because I remember trying to sit up before that, and how painful it had been. But once they'd actually sat me up, it relieved a little bit of the pain, so I was quite glad. But the actual sitting up was horrendous.

Then they had to pull me forward by my knees, so that they could get the back-board down behind me. There were people working behind through the window and from the front door and they got me onto the stretcher. I had a neck-brace on and was hooked up to drips by that stage. They put me on the back-board and covered me with a foil blanket. When you go into shock the most important thing is to keep warm. And although it was a stifling hot day, they needed to keep my body temperature stable.

There was a video which we saw in the Coroner's Court. It's just chilling. It was of the rescue team getting me out, and there was this terrible, terrible screaming.

Were you aware that anyone else was alive at that stage?

I knew that the four had died and I knew that Steven was alive because we were talking. He'd regained consciousness by then, but he'd sustained such a terrible head injury that he didn't know where he was. He thought he was in a car. So he was trying desperately to get out. And by trying to get out he was trying to push me off him. But every time I tried to move, I could feel bone grinding in my back.

I tried to keep him calm, but he didn't know where he was. One of the rescuers asked him at one stage what his name was and he looked at his watch and said, 'one o'clock'. He was completely incoherent.

Finally we were actually walked about 20 minutes through the bush to the helicopter. Then the helicopter flight was about 40 minutes to the hospital. In the helicopter I was starting to get terrible shooting pains down my right leg, but they didn't want to give me too many painkillers because other injuries could have been masked.

They didn't give me many painkillers at all and when I asked them why, they said that if I wasn't able to relay to them that I was feeling pain while they were trying to get me out of the wreckage, they could be causing more damage. I could understand that, but I would rather have not gone through it.

There's a story within the story because what was happening at home with my family and Nigel was just as horrendous. Nigel was working in the hangar at Camden Airport and he heard the mayday call because he had the radios turned on monitoring the frequencies. So he actually heard the mayday call go out. There were police around and he found one of the police to ask what was going on. They confirmed that an aircraft was having engine failure and it was going down.

He asked who it was and was told that it was ours. He knew that we were crashing. The first report was that

ACCIDENT

the wreckage had been found. Next they reported that there were people outside the wreckage and they were waving. So Nigel thought, 'Oh, thank goodness, they're OK'.

Then they said that there were some injuries and they were going to transport them by helicopter to the football oval at Camden. So Nigel went to the oval with the police. While he was there they got another report saying that there were at least two people killed and one of them was a female. There were only two girls on board, Janine and me. Then they confirmed about an hour later that there were four people dead. And so the odds were just getting worse and worse for Nigel.

The awful thing was that Nigel was very good friends with the father of the other girl and he was at the airport as well. They knew that there was one female survivor and one deceased. So they were walking past each other thinking, 'It's either going to be him or it's going to be me. One of us has lost the person we love.'

In the meantime Nigel had contacted my parents. My dad was at home and Nigel said, 'Allana has been in a plane crash. We don't know what's happened but prepare for the worst.' My father rang the rest of my family. My brother had come from the North Shore where he lives to Camden. He arrived at Camden before they confirmed what was happening. My sister was in a state of shock.

And the reports were so confusing, so conflicting. When I arrived at the hospital I kept saying to the rescuers, somebody has got to get in contact with my husband. I knew he'd be going berserk. But nobody would, because they didn't know whether or not I was going to die on the way to hospital, and they didn't know what my injuries were going to be.

So when I got to the hospital the rescuers said to the nurse, 'She's really worried about her husband, can somebody phone him'.

The hospital rang our office, but a friend answered

the phone and gave Nigel the message that I was alive. Unfortunately, the father of the other girl was close by when Nigel was told. It was just a terrible way for it to happen.

Friends were at the hospital before I even got there. I was taken into emergency and all my clothes were cut off, but that's a bit blurred because by then I'd been given painkillers and I was very dazed. I remember my mum coming in, and I remember Nigel being there, of course.

Then they took me into surgery that night to operate on my stomach because it was very swollen and badly bruised. They were worried about internal bleeding. There was a lot of bleeding but none of the organs were damaged, luckily. I've still got the lap-strap mark across my stomach. It will be there for a long time.

After five years?

Yes. The bruising took about eighteen months to go away.

They established that my leg wasn't broken, which was strange because it was completely facing the other way, so that was quite extraordinary. It was all ligament damage. But they confirmed that my back was badly broken.

It was described as 'a destructive injury'. But they were hoping that my spinal cord was just being pinched or bruised and that after surgery I might get some movement or feeling back. I went through all the pin-prick tests, as everybody does with spinal injury. They established that I couldn't feel very much in my legs and I couldn't move my feet.

I went into surgery on the 24th—it was the day before Christmas when I had the spinal fusion done. In surgery they found that the nerve endings had completely come out of the spinal column and there was a blood clot at the base of the spinal cord, which was lucky because for that sort of injury what they'd normally do is cut the end of the spinal cord and secure it. But because the blood

ACCIDENT

clot was there, they decided to leave it. If they had cut it, I would have been completely paralysed. I wouldn't have had any movement at all.

The risk was that spinal fluid could be lost and I could be quadriplegic. So it was a big decision to make. They took all the nerve endings, basically moved them up to where they were supposed to go, and hoped that they would reconnect. Then they secured the spine with self-tapping screws. Took a bit out, put a bit in, and moved a bit around.

I had to lay on my back for eight weeks and was log-rolled every two hours. I couldn't move for eight weeks. I thought it would never end. There's not much to do when you're lying flat on your back. It's very frustrating and boring. You just get wrapped up in the whole daily routine of a hospital: Woken up for a bed bath at some ungodly hour and fed dinner at 4.30 in the afternoon.

I remember my stomach was really sore after they'd taken the staples out and I said to Nigel, 'There's something wrong. I just don't feel well.' The nurse kept repeating that it was going to be a little tender for a few days. But I was certain that there was something wrong. Nigel kept asking the nurse to get a doctor. I felt something running down my stomach and when Nigel pulled the blanket back, it was clear that my stomach was infected. The wound was starting to open and there was all this gunk coming out. It was revolting.

Then the staff went into panic mode and got the surgeon straight out of surgery. One of them held me down, took a scalpel and cut my stomach open again—no anaesthetic, nothing. Then for four weeks, twice a day, I had to endure saline gauze being packed into my stomach so that the wound could heal from the inside. They'd do that in the morning, leave it in there all day, and at night they'd pull it all out, then pack it back in again. Oh, it was just awful!

I couldn't eat for about two weeks. I was on a drip. I remember the first cup of tea I had, and that was just the best cup of tea in the whole world! I drank it through a straw.

I didn't eat very much at all and lost a lot of weight. I got down to six-and-a-half stone. It's strange what happens to your body when you're lying flat on your back for eight weeks, and how things change. I remember my breasts migrated under my armpits because I was lying flat on my back for such a long time. I thought, 'I'm never going to be able to put my arms down again!'

Eight weeks is a long time to remain motionless. During that time I had to deal with so many emotions. I had lots of visitors and that helped to ease the boredom, with never-ending X-rays and tests. But at night, when it was quiet and there was no one around, all my feelings, both physical and emotional, became magnified. The physical pain was often unbearable and I usually spent the night pumped full of pethidine. It was also the time to contemplate what had happened to me and what was going to become of me. I was sometimes so scared and full of despair that I'd cry myself to sleep. I also had to mourn for the friends whom I'd watched die so tragically. I asked myself why my life had been spared and thought maybe they got the better deal.

And your family came and helped?

Nigel was there every day. He'd come in at 8.30 in the morning to feed me breakfast and stay most of the day.

When I was lying flat on my back and still in traction, it was all so unreal. But I thought from the beginning that I was going to be able to get up and walk. I didn't question it. I thought, 'They keep telling me that I'm not going to be able to walk, but I'm just going to have to lie here for eight weeks, then I'm going to get up and go'.

ACCIDENT

Who told you that you might not be able to walk?

After he'd done the spinal fusion, the neurosurgeon told me, 'The break is very severe. The damage is too great. You're not going to walk. We're going to keep you in traction and later put you into physio.' He had no bedside manner whatsoever. Later on, his assistant came and saw me and said, 'You might be able to get around a bit using Canadian crutches on special occasions. But you have to accept that you're going to spend your life in a wheelchair.'

I remember that day. My mother came in and wanted to talk to the neurosurgeon's assistant. They went into the annexe behind my bed to talk. I knew what the assistant was going to be telling my mother, and when mum came back to the bed, it was as if she was about to put me in my grave. It was horrible.

I got very angry with her and said, 'Don't you dare give up on me because I'm definitely not going to give up on myself. These people don't know me. Please don't give up on me. Don't dare give up on me!' I'll never forget that day. We were both very emotional.

Did she ever tell you what they told her?

They said that I'd have to accept life in a wheelchair and that with time and with a lot of work, on special occasions I may be able to use Canadian crutches and callipers and get around a little bit.

But essentially it was going to be a wheelchair.

Yes. So, from that point, I got really angry and wasn't the most popular person in the ward, because people kept thinking that I wasn't accepting it. I had counsellors coming and telling me, 'Look, Allana, you just have to accept that this has happened!' But I wasn't ready to accept it. I didn't want to accept it. I wanted to have a go first. I just couldn't work out why people were being so negative, because I was ready to get up and go. So I got very angry and told people off.

Do you think that anger, or this fighting spirit, was an important component in your recovery?
I think it played a very big part. You have to really want to get better. Also, in my case I had a family and friends, and their love and support was important in my recovery. I felt I had to do it for them and I had to do it for myself. Nigel wouldn't let me give up. And I had such a great life, I couldn't possibly let it end. I wanted it back. I didn't want to miss out. My love of life was a big motivator in my recovery.

What were the landmarks in your recovery?
When I first went into physio it was quite confronting because I didn't think it was going to be so hard. It was then that I realised how difficult the road was going to be. Going from being confined to the wheelchair to being able to take some steps was very daunting.

When I left the hospital I was still in the wheelchair. I'd been in hospital for three months and rehabilitation was a further six months as an outpatient. That's when gradually I started to walk. Hydrotherapy was very good for me as well. I made progress reasonably quickly and went from walking ten steps to twenty steps in one week.

The other landmark was using the Canadian crutches and eventually I started to use walking-sticks instead of the crutches. That was a landmark! My goal the whole way through was always to be able to walk without aids—without the sticks at all. And finally I got there.

This physiotherapist I was doing sessions with was really tough on me. He worked me until I was absolutely drenched in sweat. But he got me walking. He got me walking without the sticks. I did that for a while and felt really liberated, but I soon realised that without the support of walking-sticks I was going to do myself damage

ACCIDENT

within a very short period of time, because of the amount of stress on my knees and my back. It was a hard decision to make. I remember saying to myself, 'Right, I've reached that goal but I have to accept that I'll have to continue to use the sticks. That's OK'. I'd come a long way from lying flat on my back, unable to move.

When I'm at home I don't use the sticks very much, but I have to use them when I walk outside—that's for balance and support. It just takes the weight and the pressure off my back and knees, which is the main problem.

How long did you use the wheelchair?

I was in the wheelchair for twelve months, so it took a long time. I always felt self-conscious being in a wheelchair, people usually stare. It's also very restricting because often the places you need to go have steps and that made access impossible. I was never any good using a wheelchair, all the manoeuvres you need to make to go up and down gutters, over grass et cetera. I guess I didn't persist with wheelchair skills because I didn't intend relying on it for very long. When I pushed around the city and crossed a road, I would reach the gutter, hold onto a light pole or something solid, stand up, pull my chair up over the gutter then sit down and go on my way. This always got a lot of stares. Later, when I was on crutches, I used to fall over all the time. It was very frustrating. I'd take three steps and fall over. I remember a particular day when I went to the Motor Registry and I thought, 'Mm, I can probably walk in and I can probably walk out, it's not too far'. I got to the desk and I fell flat on the floor. Luckily, one of the nurses from the local hospital was there, and she just picked me up, dusted me off, gave me my sticks and I walked out. So, I retained some sort of dignity, because once I'm down I can't get up without assistance.

Nigel and I used to set little goals. We'd say, 'OK, in

a month's time we're not going to take the wheelchair to the grocery store and I'm going to walk every single aisle of the store'. Just a couple of weeks ago when we were shopping, Nigel reminded me what a big goal that had been. Now I don't even think about it.

I remember the first time trying to walk without the sticks. We were down at the hangar and I was leaning on a bit of equipment. I asked Nigel to turn around and look at me. I took three steps, tripped over and fell into his arms. But they were the first few steps I'd taken and we were just so elated because it gave us something more to hope for—it was going to be possible, and I thought, 'OK, I can't do it now but I'm going to be able to do it'.

Throughout my recovery I felt that I was going to wake up one day and it was all going to be fixed. That I was going to be back to normal again, the way I was before the accident. I used to say to myself, 'On my birthday I'm going to wake up and it's going to be fine'. And then I'd say, 'OK, exactly twelve months from the accident date I'm going to wake up and . . .'. I was completely convinced that this miracle was going to happen, it had to happen, it was meant to be.

And I remember one day, I was standing in the kitchen by myself, and for some reason—I don't even know what I was thinking about—it just hit me that it wasn't going to happen. This was it for me. I was not going to get any better. I was going to have to deal with this injury and what had happened to me. And I went to pieces—absolutely to pieces. I just fell in a heap. It was a major crisis and I was hysterical. There was nothing that triggered it—it was just something that jumped into my head and I was so frightened for myself, of myself. I had been to see a psychiatrist for insurance purposes, for my compensation claim, and I phoned him. He sent the local doctor around to see me immediately because they were worried that I was going to do something. I was frightened that I was going to do something too. I went into a deep

ACCIDENT

depression and saw the psychiatrist for months. I finally had to confront the accident and it was very hard. It took about two years to come to terms with the accident and what it had done to me. Eventually I was classified as a paraplegic with partial movement.

After the accident I had a terrible fear of flying. I was evaluating my life and what my future was going to be. Flying was one thing that I wanted back. I'd had so much taken from me and I wanted the love of flying back, I wanted my zest for life back.

Before the accident I used to go skydiving, I was flying, I was hot-air ballooning. I was just a complete adrenalin freak! I'd do anything to give myself a fright. I think I've done everything in the air that there is to do. I just loved being in the air and I wanted that back so badly, because it was such a big part of my life before the accident.

I went flying for the first time twelve months after the accident and I was terrified. I hated it.

In a light plane?

Yes.

With Nigel?

Oh, yes, I didn't fly with anybody but Nigel until I started flying helicopters. But yes, we started doing a lot of flying, and I'm flying now.

I remember the first flight I took after the accident. It was in a Chipmunk which is an old two-seater aeroplane. It's a small, light aircraft. We were coming in to land, and at one of the runways at Camden you have to come in over trees and a river. I saw the trees and I had an instant flashback . . . total. I didn't become hysterical, but I was very nervous.

The second time we went flying we flew in a high performance aerobatics aeroplane. Nigel had just finished putting the prop on it and doing some work on it. I remember halfway through the flight thinking, 'He hasn't put that prop on securely and it's going to fall off'. And I remember praying to God, 'Get me down and I'll promise I'll *never* go flying again'. It was quite irrational. But you know, it got easier and easier.

I remember we did a flight a couple of years ago out west in a little two-seater biplane. It has four different fuel tanks and to go from one fuel tank to the other the engine cuts out just for a moment. Nigel normally tells me, 'I'm changing the fuel', but he forgot to tell me and it cut out. I just freaked out. But that fear diminished over time.

I have my love of flying back again. I'm a different sort of pilot from what I was before. I'm very very cautious and very aware of what can go wrong. I went to get my fixed-wing licence because after the accident they took my licence away until I could pass a medical. My feet don't move and you have to be able to push your toes down to operate the toe brakes in an air flight. They decided they could give me my licence back, but I had to have the aircraft modified with a handbrake so I could stop the damn thing. And I thought, 'Well, I don't know if that's for me'. I don't have hand controls in my car, and would choose not to drive if I had to use hand controls. I didn't want to have to modify the aeroplanes to be able to fly.

I'd always wanted to fly helicopters, so I decided to do that. Helicopters are a completely different ball game. Luckily, you only have to be able to use the rudder pedals, so I can have a proper licence without restrictions. Helicopters are great. And I feel, funnily enough—because they're ten times more dangerous than an aeroplane—so much safer flying them for some reason. I love flying them—I can't get enough of it!

Nigel and I have our own aviation business now. The main part of the business is aircraft sales. We import aeroplanes, mainly from Russia, and we sell them here.

ACCIDENT

We sell them in Indonesia as well. So, our business takes us all over the world. We probably do three trips a year overseas. We also have a maintenance workshop which we're starting to downgrade at the moment because we've just got so much work elsewhere. Nigel does aerobatic displays around the country and overseas. He's done some international air shows in Indonesia and America. We've just come back from America where he has been flying, and he flies in Australia of course.

Do you ever worry about him?

Never. People often ask me that, because what he does is quite dangerous. But I never ever think twice about him having an accident. I don't know why I don't.

What else are you planning for the future?

I'd really like to do rescue work and fly for any of the rescue services. In the meantime the school I'm flying with has offered me an instructor's job next year if I want to do that.

You've achieved an enormous amount since the accident.

There are lots of things that we've done which I forget about. Things like a helicopter trip around the top end of Australia which was really very interesting.

And we went sailing through Holland a couple of years ago, which meant having to get onto boats, walk on narrow little walkways. We've been to Russia and—I don't know, I've done things that are difficult to do in my situation. And they have been difficult. But I got through.

Two-and-a-half years ago we were at one of the Canteen camps doing joy flights for the kids. Canteen is an organisation for teenagers with cancer. I had met one of the organisers of this camp some months before, an unbelievable person called Lace Maxwell. She was a wing-walker. Lace and I hit it off from the moment we met, and we became very very good friends. I kept thinking how much I'd love to do wing-walking. Anyway, the Canteen weekend came up and she said, 'All right Allana, up you go', and I actually went wing-walking on top of a Tiger Moth. Basically, you have a frame on top of the top wing of a Tiger Moth, and you climb up on top of the aeroplane. You've got a harness on in case you fall. So there you are, standing on top of the plane up in the sky flying around. It was an amazing experience.

Lace was killed exactly twelve months later at the same event. The aeroplane crashed while she was on top. It was dreadful and terribly sad.

So none of these air tragedies changes your mind about aviation and flying yourself?

No, we've lost count of the number of people that we've lost, and we're losing people all the time. It's something that you accept. Death doesn't frighten me. I think pain frightens me but death doesn't. And because we lose so many people it's just something you accept within the industry. It's not going to change my mind.

It's a very cliché sort of thing to say but you can get killed anywhere. And I think about these kids at the Canteen camps . . . But I remember thinking once when I was about to fly, 'Oh, God, this is the adrenalin I haven't felt for a while, and I don't know if I like it any more. Do I really want to do this?' And there was this little voice that I'd never heard before saying, 'This is dangerous and you could get hurt'. Then the feeling gradually faded. The fact is that I'm more afraid of missing out on life than getting hurt while living every moment to the full.

I'm now a commercial helicopter pilot and flying as much as I can to collect the flying hours and experience needed for the few sought-after jobs available.

4

Alex Blaszczynski

Alex Blaszczynski is Associate Professor and Deputy Director of the Psychiatry Research and Teaching Unit at the University of New South Wales.

What sort of service does your unit offer?

The Unit provides treatment and runs clinics for anxiety disorders, including post-traumatic stress disorders and impulsive control disorders. We look at post-trauma in any major accident which involves some degree of threat to life or a threat to psychological integrity, so that includes industrial accidents, victims of crime as well as motor vehicle accidents.

What are the important factors in recovery from a serious accident?

I think quite clearly that there are pre-morbid risk factors—by that I mean someone's personality, life experiences and social support systems before the accident. The person who is highly anxious, insecure, depressed, suffering psychiatric illness, involved in substance abuse, will clearly have a poorer prognosis than someone who has a very good support system, a good self-identity and a sense of security within themselves. They will have some degree of resilience, will make the best of a bad situation and continue depending on their interests and focus in life. A prime example of that, I think, in the public domain is someone such as Frank Williams of the Formula One racing team. As I understand from media reports, he was driving home quickly to catch a flight, had an accident and became a quadriplegic. He acknowledges that the contribution was his own, but because he focused and had a passion for motor racing, he threw his energies into it, and I think that provided a medium for him to aid his recovery. He had a specific purpose and pursued that quite successfully.

The nature of the accident itself is another factor: whether people feel that they contributed in part to causing the accident, whether other people had been injured, whether there was exposure to grotesque sights, whether the person believed that they were about to be killed, are all important factors in determining the outcome as well as the post-accident recovery phase. That is, to what extent they received social support, early interventions, whether they recognised early symptoms of post-trauma emerging and took appropriate steps to seek counselling.

Quite often you'll find that most of the symptoms will emerge within the first two months post-trauma, but it can be delayed for twelve months and even longer in certain situations. The person may muster certain defence mechanisms—either blocking out or denying or overcompensating for the injuries—until some time down the track when they may experience another stress, an entirely independent stress, which overwhelms them and suddenly they're flooded with post-trauma symptoms.

Post-trauma ranges anywhere from discreet psychiatric

symptoms, anxiety, or signs of depression, through to the full post-traumatic stress syndrome which includes things like hyper-arousal, avoidance behaviour and intrusive thoughts.

What sort of treatment assists them most?

There are a broad range of interventions and they should be tailored to the individual. I think the key issue essentially is a supportive environment—recognising that the post-trauma symptoms are not signs of personal weakness or psychiatric instability, but rather a normal response to an atypical situation.

The important aspect is to provide adequate education to warn the person as to the sorts of symptoms that may emerge either in the near future or the longer term, that there will be a process of numbing, denial, anger, irritability and then a period of depression as the person works through the losses which have affected them in terms of impact on quality of life, loss of limb, or loss of functioning. Or, if other people have been killed, there will be bereavement issues. So, some degree of grief counselling would be important as well.

We then look at identifying each of the particular symptoms and providing treatment interventions. For example, with intrusive memories, if there are any sorts of flashbacks, recurrent dreams, techniques such as eye movement desensitisation may be appropriate.

The other effective approaches are essentially to look at over-arousal and produce some anxiety management or relaxation-type procedures. The next step then is to look at any increase in alcohol consumption and deal with that particular issue. Use of medication is appropriate, so long as one is cautious about dependency as well. The other key issue, essentially, is to try to muster social support for the individual and look at any other specific needs the person may have.

Quite often, if there are organisational needs, that is, if the person relies on rehabilitation services, there may be a lot of anger directed—not inappropriately, but injudiciously—against people that the person perceives are not really helping them. For example, someone may perceive their employer as trying to off-load responsibility or not providing sufficient help or basically ignoring them.

One case, for example, may be that of an individual who is involved in an accident in a factory, feels that their manager is basically trying to get them back to work as quickly as possible and doesn't acknowledge the extent of the injuries or psychological trauma received. As a result, the person may be displacing their anger towards the manager. This quite often does occur where compensation for injuries sustained may be a possibility. Some people think the organisation is trying to avoid or minimise cost. But psychologically one of the key issues is to try to bring the person back to work as quickly as possible so that they don't fall into the trap of increasing anxiety and fearing going back to work. But the person may, in fact, misinterpret that as the employer trying to reduce their own costs.

It's quite clear that the longer the person stays away from work, the more avoidance anxiety is experienced and a consolidation of the fears and phobias may occur which makes it difficult for the person then to resume work six to twelve months down the track.

Is it possible not to experience any psychological trauma at all following a serious, life-threatening accident?

I think it is possible, clearly possible. At one conference, for example, there was a case study being presented of a person who was involved in an airline disaster, and it was quite clear that the plane was in imminent danger of crashing as a part of the plane had disintegrated and fallen off. And one passenger, an engineer, was essentially coping by examining the fault and writing down a description of the fault causing the accident. He then wrote a letter to his family indicating that he died happy, and to prove

ACCIDENT

that, he took a photo of himself smiling. One could argue that this is rather bizarre behaviour, but in a sense he identified the situation and was dealing with it relatively appropriately.

But what if there had been physical trauma as well?

Again, part of it really is the meaning of the trauma that the person experiences. If the person is resigned to the fact of imminent death and accepts it—he may have strong religious beliefs and doesn't fear death—then that obviously may be a protective factor which may aid in his recovery.

And if the person is left with a physical incapacity?

Obviously, in those circumstances, the majority of people would suffer some degree of reaction. I would say that virtually everyone in that case clearly would suffer some degree of psychological reaction. The question really is whether that reaction is debilitating for the individual.

And clearly, in some cases, the person's religious and philosophical outlook on life may be such that the trauma assists them in some way, that they start to put things into perspective, they realise that there are things which are important and those which are not. So it may assist them in terms of helping to deal with the future in a better way, but it doesn't negate the fact that they still may have some degree of depression, anxiety and remorse over what has happened.

One of the key issues to bear in mind about post-trauma is that quite often the more severely affected individuals tend to avoid seeking treatment. And the reason for that is that they don't want to think about the accident, they want to suppress thoughts about it, and try to push these traumatic images out of their mind, throw themselves into hard work or other areas of activity. The notion of seeking treatment clearly involves recalling the trauma and forcing the individual in a sense to confront the trauma again, so it becomes extremely painful.

And so, what you find is that the people who experience milder levels of severity, are the ones who tend to receive the most treatment and attention. The ones who are severely affected and require intensive interventions, are the very ones that tend to avoid contact, and certainly avoid any sort of screening programs for their trauma.

And what would you suggest might be the outcome for those who avoid seeking help? Might they have to seek help later on in life?

Well, that's the danger, that they may cope in the short term by becoming preoccupied, or throwing themselves into their particular work or sporting achievements or whatever, and then later on in life as they're confronted with more and more stresses or their particular goals are not being achieved, they suddenly become overwhelmed by depression and anger, irritability, substance abuse and friction within relationships. They tend to drive friends and other social support systems away, and they're at risk for suicide under those circumstances.

I think it is important to be relatively encouragingly assertive with people who are at risk of experiencing severe post-trauma to be able to offer them, on a frequent basis, the opportunity for any sort of counselling. They may reject it in the first instance, but I think with encouragement they're more likely to seek treatment and help.

Post-traumatic stress management or intervention is a fairly recent treatment. Why is that?

Well, post-trauma has been world recognised for many years. I think what highlighted the importance of post-trauma was the return of the Vietnam and World War II veterans. And the Holocaust survivors. Quite clearly these people are experiencing severe readjustment problems and psychological symptoms on return to society, forcing mental health professionals to acknowledge the existence of a problem and to deal with it.

I think the other impetus has been the feminist movement and the recognition of child sexual traumas as well, and the impact of rape victims. And people suddenly realising that individuals do experience post-trauma after a whole range of atypical life-threatening situations. The occurrence of natural disasters has also increased the recognition of post-trauma—the community was still reeling over the Port Arthur massacre many weeks later. So you can have whole communities, in a sense, experiencing post-trauma type reactions, a sense of numbness, disbelief and anger.

Counselling for post-trauma is much more easily available now than it was in the past. What did people do a hundred years ago? How did they cope without it?

Oh, quite poorly. In the past people suffered in silence, increased their alcohol consumption and suffered recurring nightmares, anxiety, depression, but didn't necessarily reveal to others what the cause of that was.

I think one of the key issues when we talk about post-trauma and how people coped with it in the past is to look at the over-inclusiveness of the concept of post-trauma. In the past people were exposed to stress situations and were expected to deal with them in appropriate ways. What's happening now is that there is a tendency to utilise post-traumatic stress disorder as a means of explaining a broad range of reactions. The term 'post-trauma' has now become so widely bandied around that virtually any stress, or any unpleasant situation, is subsumed under the concept of trauma—even to the extent that a young child losing a teddy bear is suddenly viewed as being traumatised and losing attachments, or risking separation anxiety.

So I think we really have to separate out normal expected daily stresses and people's expectations that they deal with normal stresses, from atypical, unusual major traumas which threaten life. People expect to experience problems at work or even to lose their job during recessions but you don't expect, for example, that a building is going to suddenly burst into flames, that you're trapped there with other people running around burning.

It is clear that exposure to a potentially life-threatening trauma may produce significant changes in the way a person views life and functions at all levels of behaviour. What is important is that counselling and specific therapies are available for trauma sufferers, and that these should be used as soon as possible after a traumatic event in order to minimise long-term consequences.

PART II

ILLNESS

5

Kerry Harfield

Two years after Kerry's melanoma was removed, she felt a lump in her groin and secondaries were discovered in her lymph nodes. Until then, as a former Miss Australia, a teacher of science and a wife and mother, she had led a charmed life. She told me her story while we drank coffee in the sunroom of her lovely house. A very serene person of striking elegance, her generosity of spirit made this interview memorable for me.

ILLNESS

Kerry, you've recovered from melanoma—a particularly life-threatening form of cancer and most prevalent in Australia. How did you discover you had melanoma?

I had a very simple mole-type thing on my leg, which I'd had since I was a little girl. I watched it over the years—it was a bit more raised than perhaps other freckles. Over time I thought it was changing and when I'd shown it to my local GP, he said we should keep an eye on it. This was in 1991.

Then later I happened to go into the dermatology unit at Royal Prince Alfred Hospital. I mentioned it to the doctor I was seeing and she said to me, 'I'd like the Professor to see that'. And then one thing happened after another, I was busy with the children et cetera, so I didn't see him for a while. When I finally consulted him, he took one look at it and said, 'That's a melanoma'. To be perfectly honest with you, I nearly fell through the floor. Because of my science background, I knew exactly what 'a melanoma' meant.

There are three types of skin cancers, and the most dangerous and life-threatening is melanoma. Melanoma has the ability to spread—to metastasise—to other parts of the body, so it's nastier.

I said to the Professor, 'Well, what happens?' And he said, 'It comes off here and now'. Which was wonderful because there was no thinking about it, it was just a local anaesthetic, a section of skin was removed and away it went to be analysed. When he had done this, I looked at the section in a bottle sitting on the desk waiting to be analysed, and I remember thinking, 'I think my life might have just changed direction'.

I'd never been sick in my life. I'd never been in a hospital, except to have babies, which I don't consider really as going to hospital 'sick'. Going to hospital to have babies feels like a bit of a luxury really. So I thought that if the biopsy was positive, and if it was a melanoma, I had a real problem!

And the doctor wasn't sure it was melanoma at that stage?

Not entirely. The section had to go to Pathology first, but my attitude was that if the fellow who is the Professor of Dermatology suspects it's a melanoma, I'm jolly sure it is a melanoma. It was on the inside of my leg, so it wasn't one that had been necessarily caused through lots of sun exposure, but we all sunbaked far too much as children, we didn't know any different. And our parents certainly didn't know anything different.

I had the sort of skin that went very brown, and we all lay in the sun for hours on end. How dreadful now when you think about it, but we weren't as aware of the dangers even though it wasn't really that long ago. And when you have an olive-type skin that does tan, you tend to think you're OK. I'm inclined to have the mole-type skin anyway which is more at risk, rather than having freckle-type skin. Anyhow, he said he would phone me in four or five days with the results.

And what were those days like for you?

Oh, interesting. I didn't share it with too many people. I sort of hoped that it might be OK, and because it was in August and the weather was cold, I was wearing long pants so I could hide the fact that I had a dressing on my leg.

Did you talk to your family about it?

I did, yes. I talked to my husband about it and to my mum, eventually. But I knew she'd know exactly what it meant, so I was careful about what I told her because I didn't want her to worry.

Basically I just sat on it. I was told that if it was positive I'd be referred to Professor McCarthy, the Professor of Surgery in melanoma and Executive Director of the Melanoma Unit. So I would be in good hands!

ILLNESS

If it was melanoma, the doctor explained that a wider excision—the size of half an orange—would be made in the area where the mole had been, to try to remove all the problem cells. It was hoped that none of the cells had travelled and that early intervention by surgery might mean that I'd be OK. He phoned me four or five days later to say that the results showed that it was a melanoma. I went in to the hospital to have my stitches out and was transferred upstairs to Professor McCarthy. I made an appointment and was incredibly lucky because I literally walked into a vacancy which is unusual in that particular unit of the hospital. But I said, 'Look, I'm really a bit busy next week to go into hospital', and I realise how pathetic that was. He answered, 'Not too busy to come and see me, my dear'. And I thought, 'Oh shivers . . . righto.'. And that was that. I was operated on the following Tuesday.

What did McCarthy tell you at that stage?

Before surgery he asked me if I knew what the procedure was. I said what I'd been told downstairs, but he went on to explain to me that it may need a skin graft or he said we might be lucky and he might be able to get a primary closure—in other words, pull together the pieces of skin that were left on each side of the wedge after the section was taken. He said, 'We might be able to get you back together'.

The pathology test had revealed that it was relatively small—1.25 mm in depth which is not bad, relatively speaking. And when they did the wider excision, that section was clear, so it didn't need any subsequent radiation therapy.

Did you need a skin graft?

I had the surgery and miraculously it wasn't necessary. I had a leg cast on for a month or so. It was a half-leg cast, so I could go to bed at night without the possibility of popping the stitches if I bent my knee.

I was in hospital for a week. Soon after I left hospital my children, some friends with their children, and I booked to go to a Sport and Rec camp, so I toddled off to the camp a week-and-a-half after I got out of hospital, not realising how much difficulty I was going to have with this jolly leg cast. It was quite an interesting experience. Really it was ridiculous. If I had known I would have pulled out, because I wasn't a great deal of help.

It was pretty uncomfortable and of course I was on crutches because I couldn't weight bear on it. I drove to Dubbo to the camp. I've got an automatic car so I propped up my left leg on a pillow—it was the left leg that was affected and when I think about it, it was crazy. But you know it probably did me the world of good to stretch myself then rather than sit at home wallowing in self-pity.

After that I basically went to the hospital for check-ups probably every two months or so, and then the time between appointments was extended to three months. I considered it nice to go and have a chat. I didn't have any problems and I was healing very well. I was checked over completely and any moles were closely examined. I was working as a science teacher and, of course, being a mother. At that stage, Nicole was seven and Matthew was six. I had no reason to think that I'd ever have another problem.

I remember with startling clarity that Friday morning. It was two years later, so I was into the four-monthly check-ups, 'everything is going well' and almost the 'let's forget about all this' stage. For some reason I must have wiped my hands down my leg, on an apron or something, because I had been taught how to feel my lymph nodes to check that everything was OK. And I felt a lump in my left groin which was, of course the most likely leg because it was the left leg which had been originally affected.

And it was a discernible lump?

It was a discernible lump, it felt like a little grape. I knew exactly what it meant because the Prof. had always said to me, 'You will know, they're very superficial, they're very easy to detect.' Lymph glands are not deep, they're just under the skin. And I can remember thinking, 'Yes, he's right. I do know.'

I got the children to school so fast they didn't know what had hit them. I came home and said to myself, 'Now, don't panic Kerry. Let's just lie down and compose yourself—you know what you've got to do. Let me be sensible and not panic and feel this lump.' But there was no mistaking it, there was a lump on one side and not on the other. So, I phoned the melanoma unit.

I was completely on my own. I can remember hearing my husband driving the car out as I felt the lump and I thought, 'Oh, shivers! Well, OK, let's just get yourself together.' So I rang the melanoma unit and muttered my way through the conversation. They were fantastic and I was very lucky because I spoke to this very sympathetic girl who said, 'I can hear you. I know you're there. Just when you're ready to talk, you just talk to me.' Whether she realised that I was upset I have no idea. I told her who I was very quickly and said, 'I've discovered a lump'. She told me to come in that morning but that Professor McCarthy was overseas. And I was devastated. But I knew I had to go and see somebody and I knew it wasn't a case for the local doctor.

So in I trotted. And I know this sounds ridiculous, but I had an appointment that morning to have a haircut—I needed one very badly. Something inside me said, 'I just might not get another chance for a haircut for a long time'. So I went and had my haircut and I can remember the poor hairdresser who knew me very well asking me what was the matter and I told her that I had to go into hospital and that I'd found this lump. I was quite distressed.

I arrived at the clinic and saw the assistant director of the unit. I could tell by his face that he thought what I was thinking and he sent me off within the hospital to have the needle biopsy done. I could tell by the expression on their faces as they were looking down the microscopes what they were seeing, because the microscope was in the same room, and I said to them, 'Unfortunately, I do understand a bit about what you're doing'.

Then I went back to Associate Professor Thompson's rooms and he told me that I had to go into surgery. My response was, 'Let's get rid of this'. I understand about lymph glands, that they are part of the body's defence mechanism. The glands will not work efficiently if they are affected by melanoma. So I thought, 'OK, this has travelled'. The trouble with melanoma—which I was to discover—is that it only needs one cell to travel, whereas most other cancer-type cells in the body die if just one cell travels off on its own. The melanoma cells are sticky and they're very resistant to the body's natural defence mechanism. One cell can be all you need. That's why melanoma spreads to other parts of the body quite easily.

And how common is this?

I don't think it's all that common. And I suppose its chance of metastasising, or spreading, is low again because the chances of having melanoma in the first place isn't that high, but of course melanoma is on the increase. Sun exposure when you're younger causes the reaction some years later. That's a problem when you're younger or a teenager. I think we're educating the little ones about wearing hats and protecting their skin, but I'm not sure we're getting through to teenagers. That worries me because I think there's a culture which says, 'Don't do things if they're not trendy'.

ILLNESS

Can we go back and talk about the lump you found?

Well, after they did the needle biopsy I had to have a lymph node dissection which meant removing the lymph nodes from the left leg. He gave me a sort of brief summary of what might happen later.

He said that I may suffer swelling in the future in that leg and some people do get very bad oedema, or swelling. I've been lucky there, the after-effects haven't been too bad. Summer is worse than winter, though. I have a pressure stocking which I wear for the leg that needs it. It's not too attractive but mostly it can be covered up and luckily slacks and jeans are in fashion anyway. I find it difficult because I was very used to wearing shorts in summer.

So, I had the operation and at the same time they introduced me to the idea that I would be considered for the immuno-therapy program in a trial being conducted at the hospital for melanoma patients. Because I had a secondary cancer in the nearest set of lymph nodes to the original melanoma, I became suitable to go onto this program.

The surgery itself left a very bad scarring. Rather, it's a nasty position because it's longitudinally on my leg—my upper leg through the groin area and up towards the hip. Apparently it is a very difficult operation to do from a surgical point of view. It's not the most attractive scar in the world, I can assure you, but relative to not being alive, I can cope with a scar. There aren't too many people who see that part of your body, so I can survive. But it was pretty devastating, I must say.

And by the time I had the operation done, out of the seven nodes that were removed, two had melanoma cells. The melanoma could have been there for twelve months or six months or who knows how long? But it had caused irritation and therefore bleeding into the node. So this caused the node to swell. Anyhow, I had the operation but was unfortunate enough to get a golden staph infection in the wound, so that caused me to have further surgery.

I ended up having two more general anaesthetics, one to open up the wound to put drainage in, and then one to close it back up again. So it became a bit of a joke . . . you have to see the funny side of these things. Every second Thursday I was back in theatre and it was just a nightmare both for me and my family. I went into hospital initially for seven to ten days and finally I was there for thirty-five days. I was there throughout Easter and school holidays, so friends looked after the children. Friends were very good to me; they visited and kept coming back to visit, which was wonderful because I really needed their help and support.

In view of all the surgery you underwent, was there much pain associated with that and the infection?

Yes, there was. After the second operation I had to have dressings done twice a day on the open wound, and that was extremely painful. I coped reasonably well but I have vivid memories of it not being pleasant at all, because it was a case of dressing raw flesh. But the wound had to be cleaned and dressed. It was most unpleasant. I'd given birth to two children without pain relief, but I went for the pethidine for this experience.

The hospital staff are probably used to people not coping with things, and I'm not the sort to whinge, but I used to cry, 'Oh, I can't stand this . . .'. But eventually, I came out of hospital.

Was there a time throughout this experience that you feared for your survival?

It's funny you ask that, but I don't know that I actually did. I saw it as, 'There is something wrong with my leg, my lymph nodes, and we're going to get rid of the problem, and that's it'. And yet I was surrounded by people in the hospital who were much sicker than I was in the sense that they were at a further stage of melanoma. Some of them have since died. I suppose even now it sometimes occurs to me that that could happen to me too, but I think, 'No way! That's not going to happen.' Not that I could stop it, I suppose, but I saw my melanoma as different to other people's, and so therefore I wasn't going to experience the problems they had.

I suppose I just couldn't let my guard down. I couldn't let myself wallow in self-pity because I had people depending on me and I had to get back to them. So I don't think I actually feared for my survival as such. But the last two years have been much harder than the first two—between my first operation in 1991 and the second one in 1993. I've been more conscious each time I've gone for a checkup that I'm through that one. I always expect to get a clean bill of health but I'm glad when I do, whereas previously I sort of thought I was going in for a chat and, yes, I might get looked at. But now I feel, 'Oh, thank goodness that's over'. I was lucky to be accepted onto the immuno-therapy program in 1993.

Can you tell me about the program?

It's a series of injections that are given to patients over a two-year period. It's an injection from a melanoma culture. It's actually like a smallpox vaccination and that's the way the injection is given—as an intradermal only. The skin is raised in the same way as for smallpox vaccination. The idea is that hopefully your immune system will build up its own natural immunity and recognise melanoma should it come again. In fact, I do know of someone who had a secondary melanoma removed and I understand that what they discovered was a totally encapsulated melanoma. In other words, the immune system had fought this melanoma and isolated it. It was totally encapsulated by immune tissue.

How often do you go for a check-up?

I finished the two-years immuno-therapy in June 1995 and Professor McCarthy is happy to see me now every six months.

Have you recovered sufficiently to return to work?

Yes, I went back to teaching science on a casual basis because standing on my leg was a bit of a problem to me and teaching is a standing-up profession. I tend to stand up and walk around a lot.

I'm really enjoying the casual teaching and I'm available for block relief. There are a couple of schools that I've worked for over the last two or three years and I've done Higher School Certificate marking virtually the whole time. That has been great because it keeps you informed about what's going on in education. I'm not sure I want to go back to full-time teaching because there's a lot of stress involved in the work.

One good thing to keep out of your life in the case of cancer is stress. You need a positive approach and you need to feel that friends and family find you special and think you are important. In our day-to-day lives it is very easy to get involved in all the general routine with children, house problems, school and so on and forget to look after our own well being. I feel fitness, healthy food and taking time out for myself are very important.

How important has your attitude to this illness been to your recovery?

I think it's everything, quite frankly. And yet I don't suppose I made a conscious decision about that. I'm not the sort to think, 'Now, come on Kerry. We've got to have a positive attitude.' I tend not to spend time thinking about those sorts of things. Maybe I am that sort of personality anyway. In my case it's, 'Heavens, we've got to get on and do these things'. And life is there to be lived. Some people—friends, think I do too much and maybe I do, but that's me. I enjoy my life that way. I'm not a very good stay-at-home person, I don't think. I'd rather be out there doing something. I definitely need the stimulation. And whether that stimulation comes from going and doing things with the children or whether it comes from going off and teaching at schools or whether it comes from attending meetings or whatever, I enjoy it.

I understand you've been Miss Australia. Can you tell me about that?

I went to university and did a science degree. After I graduated and was in my second year of teaching science, I was asked to help raise some funds for the Spastic Centre which also involved being an entrant in the Miss Australia Quest. I honestly felt I didn't really want to do that. I didn't see myself as a suitable candidate for a competition which I thought was all about glamour and beauty.

But it was a fundraising vehicle for a very needy and worthwhile cause so I did enter and won the title of Miss Australia in 1975. In the three years following, I continued doing public relations with Westpac Bank which was great fun, a free and easy lifestyle, travelling quite a bit and not having a set routine. But I finally decided that I really wanted to go back to teaching because I still enjoyed it. And the travelling wears thin after a while. It can become quite tiring. And so I went back to teaching.

Later on I was married. Then my daughter, Nicole, was born in 1984 and eighteen months later Matthew was born, so that put me into the mothering brigade. Well and truly.

A few years later I was employed by ABC-TV for a couple of years doing *Encounters*—which is a documentary series covering a range of subjects. The films are mostly bought from overseas, and I introduced them. The first year we did thirteen programs and the next year it was twenty-six weeks and that was enormous fun. It was a great experience to be in a different area, although I'd had some television experience at that stage, having been Miss Australia.

I've done a few morning-type programs . . . mostly interviews to do with Miss Australia awards and how the awards have changed because in my day it was the crown and robes and all that sort of regalia. I've continued to assist on selection panels for the Spastic Centre. I had a marvellous time as Miss Australia.

So, I have to say that my life has been very rich and it continues to be so. I'm very lucky. Often it takes events like those I've experienced to make you appreciate the important things in life and to disregard the trivial, which we sometimes allow to cause so much anxiety. And not being in control of events—which happens when you're ill—makes you value the decisions you can make when you're in good health. The experience has re-directed my thinking to focus on the issues that matter and to gloss over the unimportant.

6

Barbara Asgill

When Barbara—a highly energetic woman—was told she had breast cancer and must have a mastectomy, her first response was one of impatience.

Meeting her some years later, when she'd taken time off work to make us lunch and we talked in her kitchen, the impression which remained with me was still one of impatience. She exudes a joy of living and never seems to have enough hours in each day for her busy life.

My mother had breast cancer and died when she was forty-two. She'd had her breast removed four years before that. I was seventeen when she died and I remember when I went back to school everybody avoided talking about it. That was so wrong because people in those circumstances really need to talk. My father didn't have a sign of cancer but ten months after my mother died, he was dead with cancer also.

My mother was the most wonderful person in the world. She was MY mother, and the thought of life without her was unbearable. I think this is what has made me so grateful that I recovered from cancer, because I am here for my daughters and their children.

Can you tell me what your life was like leading up to the discovery that you had breast cancer?

Very busy because I've always had and always will have this enormous energy. My family are always telling me I have to slow down, and I say, 'When I just get over this then I'll slow down', but I know I never will. So, it was a very busy time then, as it is now. In fact, my youngest daughter had just announced that she was getting married and, for whatever reason, we decided that it would be a small wedding and it would be in my house. I was in the middle of redecorating—I do all my decorating myself—so I was really pushed to get it finished.

I was having a fight with the Body Corporate about trees they wanted to cut down on the property and I had a crisis in my job, so I had all of this on my plate and was very, very stressed. This was about twelve to eighteen months before I actually found that I had cancer and I have read since that sometimes a lot of stress can be the cause or the trigger. Thinking back, knowing the stress I was under, I wouldn't be at all surprised.

I've always been in travel, but at that time I was managing both a wholesale and retail travel outlet. It was quite a big responsibility. I have since gone back to being

ILLNESS

a travel consultant. The company keeps wanting me to manage offices, but at my age and with my history, I just want to enjoy my job now. I don't have anything to prove to anybody, I've done it all.

But I was under a lot of stress at that time of my life. I'd also moved house. They say that a death in the family or the death of somebody close to you, losing a job, buying and selling a house, are all high on the list of life events which cause stress. I'd been divorced for twenty years and did everything on my own, making all the decisions and bringing up my two daughters.

How old were your daughters at that time?

The girls were grown up at that stage and my first grandchild had arrived, but that was the most pleasurable thing, of course, in the whole thing—that was the star in the sky.

At the time my breast cancer was diagnosed it wasn't a lump, it was a discharge from the nipple and I first noticed it when I was in the shower. I would rub it off and then the next day it would be there again. I'm not a hypochondriac, in fact I'm more inclined to put it off, but eventually I went to the doctor. I think I might have had a yearly check-up due and thought, 'Oh, I'll ask him about that when I'm there'. But I remember that I missed the appointment because I was so busy.

A couple of days later I rang his nurse and I said that I'd missed an appointment and she said, 'Oh, well, you're going to have to wait six months for another one'. I told her that I had a bit of a problem so if there was a cancellation, I'd be grateful. She asked me what the problem was and when I told her she found me a spot, so she recognised that it could be potentially dangerous. I saw the specialist fairly quickly after that. Anyway, I didn't worry about it until I went for the next appointment. I didn't dwell on it every day and think, 'Oh, dear, I hope I don't have cancer'.

So you didn't entertain the idea that it could be breast cancer?

Well, I always used to tell myself I wasn't going to die of cancer. I wasn't going to get cancer. I was really quite sure that I wasn't going to get it. So, I didn't worry about it.

What medical tests were done at that stage?

He didn't actually do any test on my first appointment, he just examined me and I had a mammogram, but it doesn't show up on mammogram. So, when I went back the next time he said he wanted to do a nipple biopsy and a matter of days later I was in hospital having the biopsy done. And I knew that they would have the result on the Wednesday.

I was only in hospital for a day so I was back at work on Wednesday and Karen my oldest daughter—she's a psychologist—said, 'On Wednesday, do you mind if I come over and go to lunch with you, I would like to be there when the doctor gives you the result'. I think she felt more than I did that it could be cancer. But I was anxious to hear, to get it over and done with. So I rang in the morning and the nurse said that the results hadn't come in. I rang back and Karen was there with me. I spoke to the nurse first because the doctor wasn't there, and she said, 'You'll have to speak to the doctor'. I'm very sensitive, I can pick up on people's voices and that's when I started to worry at her reaction. Then she said, 'He'll call you back in half an hour'.

Now, he doesn't like to tell people these things over the phone but I forced him into it. I like to know things right away. So he had to tell me on the phone, which I know he hated to do, but he told me that it was cancer and that I'd have to go into hospital the following week for a mastectomy.

I got off the phone and burst into tears, Karen burst into tears and everyone in the office burst into tears. Then everyone said, 'Go home. Go home', and so Karen and I got in the car and we came home. We rang Leanne, my other daughter, and we told her and then we rang my closest girlfriend, Jan, and by about five o'clock the whole family had congregated at my home—the two girls and their husbands, little Nikki, my granddaughter, and my friend Jan. We were talking about it and all of a sudden I looked around the room and saw them all sitting there with long faces so I said, 'Hold on you lot, I'm not dead yet. Go on, all of you go home! I'm going to get over this. We've all got the wrong attitude.' Right from that moment my feeling was, 'Let's get this operation over and done with and let me get on with my life'.

I can remember the day I was admitted to hospital. I never felt better in my life. I sat on the edge of the bed thinking to myself, 'I can't believe this is me. I can't believe I'm sitting here and in the morning they're going to cut my breast off, and I'm supposed to be sick. I've got cancer and I don't feel sick.'

How much time elapsed between diagnosis and your admission to hospital?

It was a week later. But that didn't worry me because I had so much to do at work. I had to get my files organised for my clients—I'm very loyal to my clients. I was so busy I hardly had time to think. And I had to buy nightgowns, get baby photos of my new grandchild to take into hospital with me, that sort of thing . . .

I remember the morning after the operation, my doctor came in to see me—I can still see him standing at the end of the bed—and told me the operation had been very successful. He said, 'We've done it in such a way that if you ever decide you want to have reconstruction, it's all ready to go'. And that was the first time anyone had said the word 'reconstruction' to me. He said that people generally wait about twelve months before they have reconstruction. And so I looked around at the nurse and said, 'OK, I'll be back in twelve months to have that done'. I remember a French woman from Noumea who was in the same ward with me. She'd been advised to have a mastectomy but she wouldn't have it. They pointed me out to her, and told her that I'd had a mastectomy, that I was well and cheerful and thought my life was worth living and I certainly wasn't going to die. But she refused to have it done.

One of the nurses had a friend who had breast cancer and she wanted to arrange for me to talk to this woman to see if I could pass my attitude on to her. Apparently her friend was very depressed and felt that she was going to die. I said, 'Look, I'll talk to her gladly for you but I don't think this is something you can give to anyone else'. This is just my personal feeling, but I think it's something that's in you, it's a positive attitude about life and I don't think you can give that to anyone else. All you can do is tell them how you feel about it personally.

So you think an individual's psychological make-up plays an important part in recovery?

Yes I do. And I'm a perfectionist—I don't know if that helps or hinders. But my mother always taught me anything you do in life you should do to the best of your ability. And I'm very much like that. I put my best foot forward with everything I do. So I think perhaps that's part of it. I know that when I found out that I had cancer, I could have been one of those who said, 'Well, It's OK for me to lie down and die'. I could have said, my mother had the same thing, she had breast cancer and she died within four years. My father had cancer. I couldn't count on my two hands the number of my relatives who have had cancer. I could have easily said, 'Okay, it's my turn'. I think my younger brother and I are similar in a number of ways. He had a stroke when he was 35, a massive stroke, he was like a vegetable. He was blind, deaf and paralysed when it first happened. Even when he got his sight and his hearing back he was like a child. He had to teach himself everything again. The company he'd been working with for many years gave him three months off on full pay and then they told him if he felt well enough he could come back after three months for a few hours a day or whatever he could cope with. Within three months he was back at work full time. So maybe it's our determination. My sister is a very strong person, too. Maybe growing up without parents made us strong.

What else do you think played a role in your recovery?

One of the main things was my little granddaughter. She was two years old and my only grandchild at the time, and I adore all my grandchildren. I felt very strongly, 'They're not going to get me, I've got to watch this child grow up'. Really, that was in the back of my mind. ' Just let me get this over and done with and get back to my life. This little girl needs me and I want to be here for her.'

And having something to look forward to. I think that plays a big role. Having people that you love around you, too, and their support. But having a goal in life, I think, having something to live for. That's so important. But then, I think those things are important to people even when they haven't got a crisis or a tragedy in their lives, aren't they?

How soon after surgery did you go back to work?

I had six weeks off. When I had the operation I'd only been with this company for a short while. I hardly had any holidays or sick leave due to me so I used the few days I was entitled to and the rest of the time was without pay. I can't afford to be too long without pay. So I gave myself the six weeks and no more. Then I was back in the office.

What were your thoughts when you came out of surgery? Were you immediately conscious of being without a breast?

I can remember very clearly. My main thought was, 'I'm alive! So I don't have a breast—that's not the beginning and the end of the world'. I was sad to see it go, it's much nicer to have a matching pair. But there are a lot more things in life more important than a breast. And I was alive—that was the main thing. I'm here, here to tell the story.

Did you feel conscious about scarring? Did that worry you at all?

No, not at that time. But I have to say there have been times when I've felt self-conscious, perhaps even more particularly since I had the reconstruction, funnily enough, because I have this enormous cut across my tummy now where skin and muscle were taken for the reconstruction, a big scar, and the new breast isn't exactly the same as the other one. I don't like anyone to see me completely naked now. And I don't particularly like the look of myself in the mirror. But I'm never shy if I go to have a mammogram or anything like that and I don't worry about my daughters or grandchildren seeing it.

What made you decide to have breast reconstruction?

I just wanted to feel normal again. I wanted to be able to put on a bra and a shirt or my night-gown and not worry about the prosthesis. You have to wear a bra to wear the prosthesis, and there were times when I didn't feel like wearing a bra under my night-gown. Or, if I was gardening and wearing an open-necked shirt, I would instinctively cover my chest when I leaned over because my chest wasn't only flat on one side, it was almost a hollow. But basically it didn't worry me too much because I remember going out one day without the prosthesis. I completely forgot about it and went to visit an old lady in the hospital. It wasn't until I came home that I looked down and there I was flat on one side. And I just laughed about it.

Has it effected your sexual life at all?

No. But mainly because I've had a very considerate man who made it obvious from the word go that it didn't make any difference to him, that it wasn't important to him. I've been divorced from my first husband for many years, but had I still been married to him I think it would have been different . . . he's a different sort of man. I feel very sorry for any woman who has to contend with a man who has a bad reaction to mastectomy.

How do you deal with stress in your life? Do you tend to avoid it?

Yes. I'm much better at avoiding stress since I had breast cancer. I used to get a lot of migraine headaches which I think are caused by stress. I don't know whether it's age that helps you cope with these things better. Just in the last couple of years, or maybe it's since I've gone through menopause, I don't know, I seem to be more able to say, 'Well, so what? I'll do the best I can and it doesn't matter if it's not quite perfect.' Mind you, I still push myself very hard. Last year all through March, April, May which is our very busiest time, we were short-staffed in the office and I worked twelve to fifteen hours every day. We don't get paid overtime but I didn't do it for that. I did it simply to get through my work and so that I wouldn't let my clients down. That was stressful but it was an enjoyable stress. They say there are two kinds of stress—enjoyable stress and really painful stress, and I think that's the difference.

So the stress you were experiencing prior to breast cancer you'd describe as unhealthy or a painful kind of stress?

Yes. I look back on those times and I remember I was run down, I was thin. My marriage break-up was terribly stressful. And I did have one romance in my life after that and, if anything, the stress was worse than the marriage break-up. The other thing that I'd like to mention is that I'm very conscious of diet now. That doesn't mean that I don't eat things that are not good for me—I love chocolate cake and all those things—but I believe that all the chemicals, preservatives and pesticides that go into our bodies are extremely harmful. I truly believe that. I read a book about a doctor who cured himself of cancer when he changed to a macrobiotic diet and I think there's a lot in that. And of course there is the philosophy which says what you tell your body is what your body does. So when you're under stress your body is reacting to the stress and that can cause the cancer or the heart attack or the whatever. But if you give your body the right messages you're healthier or you can cure yourself of the illness. Of course it's much more complicated than that but I think there's a lot of truth in that belief.

Yes, but there's something about it that worries me. What about the people who share that belief but despite all their efforts, don't recover. Why do they fail?

When I think of that I think of my dear mother, because nobody wanted to live more than she did. Someone told her then that carrot juice would cure cancer and my uncle used to bring these big jugs of fresh carrot juice to her every day and she used to swallow all this carrot juice because, as I said, nobody wanted to live more than she did. But telling yourself something and believing it are two different things. So I wonder if for some people who are doing all the right things and telling themselves, 'I'm curing myself, I want to be well again', it's lip service. Deep inside, they don't really believe it. You've got to believe it in your heart as well as your head. I suppose someone like me doesn't even spend too much time thinking about it at all. When I knew I had the breast reconstruction coming up, I put myself onto a totally healthy diet. I eat sensibly anyway, food like brown rice and lots of steamed vegetables and fresh fruit and whatever . . . the occasional piece of chocolate cake. I have never smoked and I drink very little—just a glass of wine occasionally with a meal. I exercise but I don't do enough, I always seem to be too busy. But I exercised more and I learnt meditation. I meditated every day for months, preparing myself for the reconstruction, because I thought, 'I've got to give my body the best possible chance'. And it was so successful that when I went back for my examination and told the doctor how wonderful it was that it felt like my normal breast, he said, 'You'll never have feeling back in that breast', and I said, 'But I do'. He replied, 'You couldn't possibly'. And I insisted, 'But I do. If I touch it or scratch it, I can feel it.' Neither the plastic surgeon nor my specialist believed me. In fact, my doctor tested me to see if I was telling the truth. He said, 'You turn your head away, I'll scratch across the breast and you tell me when I'm touching you', and of course I told him every time. He said, 'I can't believe this. I even did a couple of dry runs to try and trick you because I thought you could see my finger moving.' So they agreed that I had normal sensation in that reconstructed breast.

How was the breast actually reconstructed?
I have a gigantic cut across my tummy, they call it 'the bikini line' but it's really a bit higher than that, basically from one hip bone to the other. A piece of flesh, skin, and muscle was taken out. I like to describe it as a wedge of watermelon, because that's what it must have looked like. And they cut what's called a free-flap and the flesh was moved into the position. Microsurgeons and a plastic surgeon joined the blood vessels to those in the breast area. I lost my bellybutton, they had to make an artificial one for me, so I don't have a real one any more. I could never put myself through it again, it is a very big operation. I was seven-and-a-half hours on the operating table. And it was actually very painful. It was even hard to walk properly for a long time. It was certainly as painful as the mastectomy. But I remember a few years after I'd had this

reconstruction done, the doctor's nurse rang me and said, 'We have another lady who is considering it, and she has asked if she can speak to someone who has had it done, would you speak to her?' I agreed, so she phoned me. We've actually become very close friends since. When I first spoke to her I remember thinking, 'Now, I've got to be very careful I don't influence this lady one way or the other. I've only got to give her the facts and she must make up her own mind.' So I finally told her that knowing what I know now after the surgery I wasn't sure if I'd ever have it done again. On the other hand, I'm very glad it's been done because I look and feel normal again. Anyway, she decided to go ahead with it, I've seen her reconstruction and it looks unbelievably good. I was, I think, the third woman in Australia to have this type of reconstruction done, and since then of course it's been perfected.

Finally, since your recovery from breast cancer what sort of life do you lead?

Still very busy. I have a good life. I have two beautiful daughters whom I love and adore and I'm very close to them. I have a nice man in my life. I have five wonderful grandchildren who are the apple of my eye. I have a full-time job which I enjoy. So, I don't have too bad a life. I love to sew. I love to cook. I love to garden. The only problem in my life is that I don't have enough money for all the things I want to do. And I don't have enough time for all the things I want to do. But I am happy.

7

Christina Brock

Christina was diagnosed with Ewing's Sarcoma, a form of bone cancer, but after a long, painful and difficult journey of recovery, a barely discernible limp is now the only outward sign of her former illness.

I was thoroughly engaged by her fine intellect, keen sense of humour and the intimacy we shared.

Can you take me back to when you first noticed symptoms and started thinking that there might be something wrong?

It started in May 1979 when I went walking for a weekend with friends to the Royal National Park. I was nineteen. When I came home from my walk I had pain down my right leg so the next day I went to my doctor who said I had sciatica and prescribed bed rest. I followed his instructions and had a couple of days in bed and my pain went, and the next few months were fairly normal and ordinary.

However, my pain came back a couple of months later, in August 1979, with a vengeance. I'd changed doctors so I went along to my new GP and he basically said the same thing but he X-rayed my back and found there was a shadow on my sacroiliac joint. He then sent me to a rheumatologist, who looks after back and joint pain, and she just thought I had an infection in the joint and treated me with anti-inflammatories.

But the pain didn't really resolve. I was in my second year of a science degree at university, coming up to exam times, and had a few more really pretty terrible nights of pain which my family found very distressing.

I remember Dad sitting up with me one night and I was just taking Codis, or something quite simple, for pain relief and it was not having any effect. This prompted me to take it one step further and so I was admitted to hospital.

I had further tests, bone scans and CT-scans and again it was all unclear about what was going on. The focus was very much on something fairly minor which would be resolved very quickly. Anyway, I was still quite happy with that and just sort of floating along. I hadn't been in hospital before. I hadn't been sick at all, other than the normal childhood diseases.

I remember my mum leaving me that first time and wondering what I was supposed to do because I felt fine except for a bit of pain. It was a very alien environment. I was in a ward with lots of older people, lots of ladies who had rheumatoid arthritis, so I felt like a fish out of water.

Having spent four weeks there my doctor decided that I should have a biopsy of the joint. The orthopaedic surgeon came to see me a couple of days before the surgery. It was the beginning of the weekend and I was going home for weekend leave. As you can imagine I'd planned every second of my weekend away from hospital, so I was pretty off the planet. He sat me down and said, 'Sometimes we find things which we can't cure', and basically he was telling me that he thought I had cancer, but it went straight over my head, and he went on his way.

So you had no idea how serious it might be?

None whatsoever. And no one seemed particularly worried or thought it was really serious.

So, I had my surgery and I was quite ill after the anaesthetic because some bone surgery had been involved and I was given some painkillers which were making me quite sick. I don't really remember being told that I had cancer, but my parents assure me that they made the decision that they would tell me and they turned off my painkiller drip and apparently I came back to the land of the living. And they told me I had cancer, but I just don't remember that. It was a gradual realisation over the next few days, and I'm sure I was probably in denial mode and overwhelmed with the shock of it all. I had Ewing's Sarcoma which is a type of bone cancer.

How did your family respond to the diagnosis?

My brother told me later that it was the first time he'd ever seen my father cry. Andrew is four years younger than me, and then I've got two younger sisters. Mum had called Dad from the hospital to say that I had cancer and he came home and told my brother and sisters. So obviously the family was just reeling and I'm sure there was lots of communication going back and forth between my family and the extended family.

The next step on the medical roundabout was more tests and waiting for an oncologist who would come and talk to me and give me a little bit of chemotherapy. Then I could get on with my life.

It was that sense of, 'OK, yes, this has happened. I have to take some time out but it will be over really really quickly'.

And was it?

No, no, it went on for a number of years. My treatment was very intensive. I had chemotherapy for nineteen months and that had its ups and downs. I spent short periods in hospital where I'd have septicaemia, but most of my treatment was as an outpatient.

Because of my treatment regime I decided to withdraw from my university course, so I was very isolated and alone and I remember spending long periods of time at home with my brother and sisters at school and my parents working.

I think that's where I developed my love of radio and lying in bed listening to it. There are great programs on ABC Radio National, very comforting, and it's much more interactive than watching television where you can just sit and let it wash over you.

And it's also a link with the outside world because as a patient you just feel totally removed, you feel cocooned from the rest of the world, and isolated. And as a young cancer patient I think those feelings are pretty overwhelming at times, you just don't believe that anyone else has ever been through it other than old people, and they're the sort of people that you see in hospital because they're the majority of cancer patients.

ILLNESS

How did the cancer respond to chemotherapy?

I had chemotherapy for six months but then my cancer started to regrow which is quite common. But this news was like a kick in the stomach as I thought I was winning the battle and then suddenly I had the stuffing knocked out of me. Dad picked me up from hospital on his way home. It was my grandmother's night to have dinner with us so Mum was trying to feed the family, look after my grandmother and cope with this desperate news that the treatment had stopped working and that sense of trying to maintain a normal life. I think for a carer or a parent, it's as bad if not worse than for the patient, who gets a lot of attention and support. But the family is really left to carry on.

Did you suffer side effects from the chemotherapy?

Yes, the usual ones such as nausea, vomiting, and I lost my hair. I was told that it would happen. I remember I was really really distressed because, when I'd have a shower, great handfuls of hair would come out. But once it was gone it was gone and I just wore scarves but I had a couple of weeks which I absolutely hated. I also felt compelled to educate people around me that I was bald, so I'd whip my scarf off in public and shock people. I think I looked OK bald and my friends used to say I looked great so that wasn't a huge problem.

I lost lots of weight, that was a problem. Another side effect of my chemo was infertility. At the time of my treatment this wasn't an issue, but it was when I went into remission and I wanted to start my life up again.

Did you take hormone replacement therapy?

No, not for a few years. In fact, part of my recovery process was dealing with issues such as HRT and another was pain which I still had for many years after my treatment finished. So I did the round of the pain clinics and finally that was resolved and it's basically gone now. It was pretty amazing.

So you mean that even though you went into remission the pain didn't go?

No. The radiotherapy damaged the nerves so there was a lot of scar tissue. While the cancer was gone, the nerves had been damaged. But amazingly the pain disappeared with time.

Once I'd dealt with my infertility in that I got information about what was available—IVF and all that sort of thing—I really was able to accept it and put that experience into perspective. And that was a very important part of my recovery, just accepting the physical changes to my body. I did have some pain and I couldn't play tennis any more, I couldn't walk for long distances or if I went to an art exhibition I couldn't stand for two hours. And I couldn't have children. But in a way I coped with my physical 'disabilities' by getting information.

I remember your saying when we first met that your friends were terrific, they were very supportive, but you'd occasionally get strange responses from some people.

There was one girl at university who was initially quite supportive of me, but maybe she just found my cancer experience too confronting. My other friends whom I'd known longer were able to deal with the experience and support each other, but she was really quite scared and the friendship ended even though we'd been fairly close for eighteen months at university. In fact, contact with my university friends dropped off but my school friends supported me through the experience. They had a memory of me before cancer, so they could handle it.

Did you ever question that you may not survive or were you always confident that you would survive?

Twelve months after I was diagnosed I had a really severe bout of septicaemia which is a systemic blood infection. The bone marrow, hair follicles and gut mucosa are made up of rapidly dividing cells and so are very sensitive to the effects of chemotherapy. That's why cancer patients often get infections, hair loss and mouth ulcers.

It was just before Christmas in 1980 and we were having Christmas up north. While Mum had stayed in Sydney with me because I had to have some treatment, my dad had taken the rest of the family on holiday and Mum and I followed a week later. When we arrived there I remember her being very angry with me because I felt ghastly and I was just lying around watching the cricket on television and not really participating in the holiday.

Anyway, I became more and more ill and started to bleed from my bowel. I can remember my brother carrying me to the toilet and then I started to fit. As Mum works in Special Ed. she'd seen someone have a fit, so she went and got the local doctor who called an ambulance and they took me to nearby Kempsey Hospital. I had an incredibly low haemoglobin of 2.4, a raging temperature and I was bleeding because I had low platelets. So they stabilised me and got me over a real hump. I think that was a point where I could have died, it was really pretty touch and go. The following day I was flown back to Sydney by air ambulance and the family followed by car. I was discharged from hospital just before my twenty-first birthday and had a couple of parties, but I was really withdrawing from everyone around me.

At this point in time I felt depressed and isolated. I just didn't feel I belonged anywhere. I couldn't relate to my friends, they were getting on with their university courses and going overseas and starting careers. I felt out of control—going through those feelings of, 'Why me? Why is this happening to me and not someone else walking down the street?'

I got angry after the depression lifted. At the time I was starting to accept the changes which had happened to me both physically and emotionally. Those feelings of not belonging continued for a long time where I couldn't relate to people around me. I felt much older than my peers and going back to university was really difficult.

Anyway after this bout of septicaemia I decided I didn't want to have any more treatment. I thought the cure was worse than the disease and couldn't see an end in sight. Mum and Dad accepted my decision which was really hard for them because I was really making a decision to die. However, that's what I felt I had to do. So I had a few months off until my oncologist called me. Lots of other people from the hospital had been calling me, but I just refused to speak to them.

When my oncologist called we negotiated that one of the drugs would be withdrawn and I would have a few more courses of treatment. I finally felt I had some control. The oncologist and I had come to a mutual decision rather than my being told what to do. I went into remission six months later in 1981 and have been there ever since.

What did remission actually mean to you? Was there a day that you remember?

No. I can't even remember the date that I finished chemo. And, in a way, that period after the treatment finished was a difficult one because all my formal support with the hospital was cut off and suddenly I was seeing my doctor every six weeks and then every three months. I'd built up close relationships with the oncology pharmacist and also some nurses in the chemo day clinic and suddenly all that was gone. I was on my own at home doing nothing.

What was the process of getting back into the world? Into relationships and a meaningful life?

I finished chemo in June and I went overseas for four months. I felt that it was really important to try to re-establish my independence. It was a bit of a disaster because the girl I went with was pretty unprepared for how ill I still was, mentally and physically. Fortunately I had my cousin and his wife in London and I spent lots of nice times with them. They looked after me and cared for me and I did some travelling as well.

However, when I came back to Australia everything I'd left—my unhappy life—was still there waiting for me. So I moved out of home in 1983, got a part-time job and did a few courses, some cooking and took French lessons. And slowly just tried to re-establish my self-confidence, establish the person that I'd been before I got sick, which had been forgotten.

Apart from your immediate family were there any key people around who helped you re-establish your life?

There were lots of people who came into my life briefly who gave me confidence, both male and female. However, I really didn't have any close relationships with men for a long time—part of that was accepting my infertility and separating it from my sexuality which tended to get a bit caught up together. Often, when you're in great need, you meet key people who give you what you need at the time. And I've met a string of those people.

In 1985 I finally completed my science degree. Then I got a job quite quickly, which was really good, and began establishing a normality in my life—being like everyone else, you know, which was what I longed to be. But I still felt very, very isolated and quite depressed. I still had a lot of pain and just didn't feel like a twenty-six year-old felt, whatever that was. My healing was a very gradual process.

In 1989 I was one of a group of people who set up CanYA. It was a support group for people with cancer aged between twenty and thirty-five years and their carers. At that time, CanYA gave a focus and a meaning to my experience. I'd been involved with a cancer support group at the hospital since '82, but very much as a participant rather than an organiser. However, setting up CanYA gave me an outlet and allowed me to validate my experience.

Since then you've obviously had a very busy life, working as a scientist and running CanYA. What is the work that you do?
I'm a scientist with a degree in the biological sciences—microbiology and biochemistry majors—and a Masters in immunology. I've been working at Royal North Shore Hospital for nine-and-a-half years in the immunology lab which offers a clinical service to the inpatients and outpatients in the hospital. And I've also done some medical research.

CanYA takes up a lot of my time and I think I'm getting to a stage where I'd like to wind that down. However, the organisation is unfunded and I'm not prepared to take my leave without securing some funding. I can see that CanYA is beneficial by providing peer support in the form of a newsletter and bimonthly meetings, and a volunteer visitor service. However, I think you get to a stage of your life, which I am reaching, where I want to put my cancer experience in the past. Though I think I will always have a link with cancer support networks.

I will always do some community work as I really like that sort of thing, and perhaps that is my way of giving back something to the community. That may well be just a facet of my personality which has been developed through my cancer experience.

One of the important issues CanYA deals with is infertility. Can you talk about the impact it had on you?
I remember asking my oncologist if I had any choice about treatment. And I remember him saying quite frankly, 'Well you can be fertile and dead, or infertile and alive'. As I have said, when I was having treatment there was so much happening it just wasn't an issue for me at all. But once I went into remission and was trying to re-establish myself again, dealing with post-menopausal symptoms like hot flushes was a reminder of what had happened to me. At

that point I was angry about the unfairness of it all. My friends were just starting to get married and have children, and I was feeling very abnormal and out of it.

And how did you come to terms with it? What information were you given?

I went on a journey to find an empathetic doctor—which took me a long time. It wasn't until 1988 that I eventually found a female doctor who helped me sort out my hormone replacement therapy and referred me to a gynaecologist. She didn't really give me sexual counselling but was very empathetic and really helped me understand what was going on with my body and accept what had happened. She gave me as much information as I needed about IVF, which is often just what people need. They don't need any more than that.

So is IVF a real option?

Yes. In my case it is, as I have two sisters. One can donate an egg to me. So there's that genetic link, rather than from a donor who's totally unrelated genetically. I don't know that I'd put my body through that process, but it's an option. And in a way, being thirty-five, I've got lots of friends who are single with their biological clock ticking away. So there's a real urgency for them to find a partner. But I feel removed from that because I guess I've made a decision that I won't have children. And I feel quite comfortable in being able to nurture in other ways rather than that physical process of giving birth to a child. In a way, I feel that it's positive, when I see my friends scrambling and getting a bit hysterical about it all.

How has an illness such as you've experienced affected your outlook on life?

I think an experience such as mine enables you to re-evaluate your priorities in life and, while I don't pretend to be able to escape the mundaneness of life, I think usually

I can take a step back from what's going on and really see what's important to me and leave aside all the humdrum.

Basically, material objects are less important, and my relationships with people and my CanYA work are what I think life is all about. I'm probably less materialistic than a lot of my peers, although a lot of that has to do with my upbringing. So I think it's very hard to separate what is the result of my upbringing and what is the result of my cancer experience because I was only twenty when I got sick.

My family are important to me. And I have a need to make a mark. I don't mean being famous but, I suppose, leaving a legacy or giving something back to humanity. It might be something that may not ever be recognised formally.

Part of the reason that I've stuck with CanYA is that I had such a difficult time during my treatment and recovery that I'd like to make it easier for other people. I know I would have benefited from talking to someone, and it's such a simple thing to do.

I suppose I feel special in having survived, too. Survivor guilt is a well-recognised phenomenon and certainly, in the initial stages of my recovery, I really wondered why I was still alive.

Can you tell me more about survivor guilt? At the time of your treatment did you get to know young people who died?
Yes I did. I had a fantastic charge-sister in my chemotherapy ward who had insight into what I was going through and could really empathise. She was my mum's age and I've kept in contact with her over the years. It's really good for cancer survivors to maintain contact with people working in the cancer field, because it's really tough for them. They deal with lots of patients some of whom die. While there are lots of cancer survivors, you don't tend to go back to the places where you were treated, so health professionals tend to get a very jaundiced view of cancer.

Anyway, Jane introduced me to other young people because she could obviously see that I felt very isolated. But all of those people died, so I didn't have any survivor role models.

I think I really grappled with survivor guilt after I went into remission. When I was trying to deal with what had happened to me and make sense of it, wondering why it did happen, I think the answer is, Why wouldn't it happen to you? Why not? It's a very simple answer but not obvious to everyone. I don't think there's a God up there saying, 'You've been bad, you're going to get cancer'. It's just a question of genetics and bad luck.

And is why some people survive while others die an impossible question to answer, taking into consideration all the variables, including genetics?

Yes. It's very complicated because it's not as simple as having a positive attitude. It is said that you can cure your own cancer, but if you take that a step back it then means that you've caused your own cancer. And that's such a burden. People do die of their disease. I think survival is related to how we respond to treatment, our age, the sort of support you get. There are lots and lots of factors which determine the outcome.

8

Stewart Dunn

Stewart Dunn is Professor of Psychological Medicine, a conjoint appointment between the Royal North Shore Hospital and the University of Sydney.

Can you talk about the studies you've done with people who recover from breast cancer and melanoma?

These studies date back about nine years ago, when we looked at the possibility of measuring psychological aspects of patients' adjustments to cancer which may have had an impact on their survival. Six years ago, with Professor Alan Coates, who is Research Director of the Sydney Melanoma Unit, we commenced a study to look at psychological function in patients with primary or advanced melanoma or breast cancer.

From the time of diagnosis, and for the first two years, every three months we measure the stress patients experience because of cancer, how serious they perceive it to be, and the method by which they cope with cancer at every time point—their emotional adjustment to cancer, in other words; whether their anxiety about cancer is mediated by their coping response. And their social support in respect of information, emotional support and practical support from doctors, family and friends.

We measure those factors for the first two years, then we continue to follow the patients and at the end we will look at the number of patients with primary disease who relapse, and the number of patients with advanced disease who die. We will then be able to see the way a person experiences cancer, copes with cancer, feels about cancer and gets support in dealing with it; the way that affects their survival from the point when they're initially diagnosed, or how that changes; and whether dramatic changes in any one of those factors affects survival.

One would presume that psychological factors, if they influence cancer, can influence it in two ways. The first is a behavioural pathway, so that if a lot of things work well for you, and you feel that you have things to do and you feel that you're empowered, then you have some control and seek out the best treatment. You will always attend your treatment, you'll go right through to the end of treatment. So by doing those behavioural things you increase the chances that you will receive the best treatment and stay with it and survive longer.

Then there is an immunological pathway which suggests that the way you think about cancer affects your immune response—your body's ability to fight the cancer. And that's why we think coping is probably not going to be the critical factor; it's more likely to be the emotional response, because the emotions are about hormones, and they're much more closely linked with immune mechanisms than is the mechanical way you choose to cope, like reading books about cancer or talking to people about it.

However, there are difficulties with immune measures. If you showed that natural killer cells are decreased in the blood of patients with a particular cancer at a particular time, that's not to say that they're not concentrated in a particular target organ, because you're only sampling from the blood. So it's one aspect or one change that you're picking up and you don't know what's happening elsewhere.

There's consistent evidence that stress mechanisms can affect immune response in terms of animal models. One of the interesting studies was one in which mice were implanted with an osteo-sarcoma. They'd previously been exposed to a learned helpless-type situation where they were involved in some experimental set-up so that no matter what they did, they could not affect outcomes—which might be getting food or avoiding a small shock. So there was one group of mice which were trained to be learned helpless, and another group which were not trained to be learned helpless. And the sarcoma grew much more quickly in the learned helpless group and more of those animals died faster, quite significantly faster.

So there are animal models that suggest there is an immune cancer growth mechanism, and there are animal models which suggest that there is a stress immune response mechanism. There are also human studies which look at stress and immune response.

There is little doubt that immunological response affects tumour growth. There was a study where patients with melanoma were encouraged to talk about and ventilate their anger. It was found that in those patients who ventilated their anger, natural killer cells were elevated.

What other study, or studies, have revealed important data about recovery from cancer?

Our study arose because there was a famous report which came from the Royal Marsden Hospital in England. Beginning in the late 1970s, they followed a cohort of sixty-two women with breast cancer. The women were interviewed by psychiatrists soon after they were diagnosed, and the psychiatrists categorised their coping strategies into, for example, Fighting Spirit, Denial, Stoic Acceptance and Helpless/Hopeless. Each patient was interviewed twice by a different psychiatrist so that they could establish the reliability of the categorisations of the psychiatrists, and that was fairly impressive. It came out with a correlation of about 0.8 on a scale of 0 to 1 where 1 is perfect correlation. So the psychiatrists were able fairly consistently to categorise the initial way these women coped with a diagnosis of breast cancer.

They did no more intervention, no more measurement with those patients, but five years later counted the number of women who had died, then at ten years and then at fifteen years. They published those results in *The Lancet*, which is a prestigious medical journal, and it received a lot of attention.

What they found was: at five years, ten years and fifteen years, women who showed Fighting Spirit initially, and women who Denied, were more likely to be alive than women who showed Stoic Acceptance initially or who were Helpless and Hopeless. And that in itself is interesting because, whilst they didn't analyse it in this way, when you think about it, Fighting Spirit and Denial are holding cancer at arm's length—in other words you don't accept that you have cancer, you fight it and you keep it outside, you deny it. You might do lots of very practical things, like collecting lots of information, if you're fighting. You might carry on as if you don't have the cancer if you're denying, but they are certainly externalising ways of coping psychologically. Whereas, to Stoically Accept or to become Helpless and Hopeless, you have to accept that you have cancer, and they are internalising strategies.

Now, the problem with those studies, from our perspective, was that we knew nothing about how stable that Fighting Spirit was, because they only measured it at the time the women were diagnosed. We didn't know whether it changed. It could have changed dramatically. It was also a small sample and it's very difficult to extrapolate from sixty women.

Another problem was that a number of intervention

studies already started to emerge after the first of *The Lancet* publications where people said, 'Well, OK. Let's try and intervene and shift to a Fighting Spirit because that will increase patients' chances of surviving.' But if it's part of the natural history, for whatever reason, of breast cancer, that women who fight initially survive longer, it does not necessarily follow that inducing Fighting Spirit in women who don't naturally respond that way will have the same effect.

It may be that the initial response is something intuitive that is also associated with immunological or other physiological responses. So, just changing the coping strategy may not guarantee the same result. Therefore we decided that what we needed to do first before we go along any sort of intervention pathway, is to establish the natural history of women adapting to breast cancer.

We have not yet followed enough women with breast cancer for long enough in our study to have the statistical power to conduct the survival analysis, but we do with the melanoma patients—particularly those with advanced disease. Since Alan Coates had a close association with the Sydney Melanoma Unit, and melanoma was the other major cancer that affects Australians—in fact, it has the highest incidence of melanoma in the world—we decided to do the same thing with melanoma patients.

Advanced metastatic melanoma is a fairly lethal disease and of the 119 patients in the cohort who have been followed for six years, 77 have died. We know all the medical and biological characteristics of those patients and, when you put them into a survival analysis, you can control for all the factors. We also put in their age, gender and other demographic factors which we know are important in predicting survival in metastatic melanoma.

The patients who said, 'I believe this treatment will cure me', survived twice as long.

ILLNESS

And that was at a terminal stage of the disease?

That's right, so that's a *big* difference. It's certainly an important component of living with a disease like metastatic (or advanced) melanoma.

Is it correct then to say that we haven't established a personality type that is more likely to get cancer or survive cancer?

I think we are a lot closer than we were two years ago. There was a meeting held at the University of Melbourne in 1992, called The First Slezak Cancer Symposium. The symposium was titled, 'The Psyche and Cancer'. It was put together by Gabriel Kune, who is a surgeon, and Susan Bannerman, a psychologist. The conclusion reads: 'I believe we have a lot of anecdotal and observational evidence and a small but increasing volume of well conducted controlled studies, both retrospective and prospective, which give us a basis for the view that the psyche does have a role in the development of malignant tumours. There is also a small, but increasing volume of sound evidence that there are plausible biological mechanisms which can explain this connection.'

An interesting cross-section of very experienced and senior surgeons, oncologists, psychiatrists, psychologists, psychotherapists and plastic reconstructive surgeons, were assembled for this symposium and were asked to talk about their own anecdotal experience of the relationship between the psyche and cancer.

There were some fascinating insights. For example, Gabriel Kune began by saying, 'In a surgical practice spanning 25 years, I have personally been involved with the management of 5000 patients with cancer particularly of the gastrointestinal tract, and of the breasts. Of these I can recall not more than twelve people who had a particularly and medically unexpectedly long survival in the face of an advanced cancer.'

He concluded, when he summarised special characteristics of the long survivors with advanced malignancy, 'First they seek a wide exposure to conventional medical opinion and treatment. There are lots of clues. They take control of their own health. They'll sort out for themselves what they want and what they don't want, and they are often critical of their medical management.' They're pains in the butt. Secondly, they seek a wide exposure as well to non-conventional therapies, so they look for alternative unconventional management.

And, in fact, in our research with cancer patients attending Royal Prince Alfred Hospital in Sydney, about 50 per cent of those use at least one alternative therapy as an adjunct to their conventional treatment, at an average cost of about $500 to $600.

Kune said that thirdly, 'They operate at an intuitive level'—they're not thinkers, they're doers; they're not intellectuals, they operate at a very intuitive level. And they use that intuition to guide their decisions.

And then, fourthly, he said, 'You often get a sense of tranquillity, peace and spirituality when you're with these people, they're not at all afraid'. Now, they are interesting observations.

Were the twelve patients he cited in the advanced cancer category?

Yes, these were patients with advanced malignancy.

In anecdotal terms I can actually confirm and echo his sentiments. I remember seeing one woman who had been at death's door three times, and each time the family was told she wouldn't survive the night, but she pulled back. When the cancer relapsed, she came to see me because she was finding it a little more difficult to cope, and I found her just remarkable. She did have a sense of peace. She had also been meditating most of her life and she meditated because that asserted how she felt life should be lived. She didn't do it because that was the way of managing the cancer. It was almost as if the cancer was incidental.

I've looked at a lot of international studies about recovery from cancer and even then it's the tip of the iceberg, but many of them are contradictory in their results.

Absolutely. When you do a med-line search on psychology and oncology you get hundreds of references. I did this two years ago for a national breast cancer consensus conference. When I did that literature search, questions like 'Why people delay in presenting when they have symptoms of cancer' were getting a lot of research attention. The extent of psychological disturbance associated with having cancer was at the top of the list.

There were a lot of issues about genetic aspects of cancer. Right down the bottom of the list were psychological factors affecting survival. So it actually got the least attention. Presumably that is because to get any useful information you're talking about large-scale studies and long-term follow-up.

It seemed to me that the methodology was often a problem in these studies.

The methodology has been shocking actually. The early studies were small with maybe thirty-five patients with a variety of different cancers. The instruments that they used to measure physiological adjustments were poor, and there was no control for differences in the type of cancer, the severity of cancer or nodal involvement.

Then there were conflicting results. One study of a small number of patients used a symptom check list, the SCL90, which is a standard instrument. In stage III/IV breast disease, they found that patients who expressed a lot of anger, ventilated their anger and expressed their emotion, survived longer. A study published two years before found the complete reverse—that patients who expressed no anger do better.

The Memorial Sloane-Kettering Cancer Institute published one of the first larger scale studies of well over 200 patients with breast cancer and found that the symptom check list didn't predict anything. And that's why this study of ours is going to be important because it's taken a lot of investment of time and energy and a lot of patients.

There seems to be, rightly or wrongly, a belief in the community that if you experience major stress—through a marriage break-up, the death of someone close to you, or whatever—you are more at risk of developing cancer. There is also a very popular view that if you do have that fighting spirit, if you face your cancer, and you decide that you're going to get on with your life and survive, that you're very likely to do so.

Now, it seems to me that those propositions have still to be proven. Would you like to comment on that?

There are studies which have tried to look at life stress and show that it might be related to the onset of cancer.

You can't feasibly do the definitive prospective study because you would have to measure people's life stress generally across a population and then look at cancer risk. But now that the breast cancer gene has been identified, if you find a family who have the breast cancer gene, then you can actually look at life stress in all the women in that family who are exposed to a higher risk, and see whether life stress in that population prospectively has anything to do with the onset of cancer.

And that would be consistent with the findings in insulin-dependent diabetes where it's now fairly well established that there's a specific genetic component which, given the stress of some environmental trigger like exposure to Rubella, and other triggers, will cause the insulin-dependent diabetes to develop. Having identified the breast cancer gene, it may well turn out that there is some sort of environmental trigger.

It may well be that life stress is a sufficient trigger to precipitate diabetes or cancer in a person who has the right genetic predisposition.

And the general perception in the community that people who have great determination and fighting spirit have a better chance of recovery. Can this be proven?

It's not proven. I don't know whether you can ever prove it, again, unless you look at prospective randomised studies. If you had a randomised study where you took one group of women and intervened, then took another group and didn't intervene, and it showed a difference, then that would be much more indicative that there is a cause-and-effect relationship.

A study published in *The New England Journal of Medicine*, took a fairly substantial group of women with breast cancer who were randomly assigned to a support group or to routine care.

In the support group they talked together about dying and about their feelings. The women who had been in the support group actually reported a much better quality of life and psychological adjustment. Then they were followed up to find out who had survived and it was found that the median survival was nineteen months in the control group and thirty-six months in the support group.

So that was one study where women were randomised and were given a chance to talk about it, think about it and draw strength from each other. The kind of conclusion from that is that strong emotional support can improve your chances of survival.

There is a kind of consistency in the anecdotes and in the experiments and research—however flawed they all are—that says that there is a group of people who show some sort of composite of either fighting or consistently looking on the bright side, seeing the glass as half full, who do better.

Optimism is an interesting thing. In our studies we've asked patients, immediately after a consultation, 'What is your diagnosis? What is the treatment? What is the treatment intent? How widely has this disease spread? What are your chances of being cured?' And we ask the medical oncologist exactly the same questions. So, we've had an objective statement of what the patient had been told compared with what the patient said.

Results showed that only 17 per cent of patients got correct the probability that they would be cured according to the objective standard of their doctor. As you'd expect, there was a huge optimism bias. Most people see their survival as longer than their treating doctor sees it.

So when people like Kune recall twelve or more patients who survived much longer than expected, what he expects is quite different from what patients expect. So optimism is an interesting thing.

Some people say it is denial. There is a lot of literature about men who deny that they've had a heart attack—getting down on the floor and doing push-ups to show that they haven't had a heart attack. Men who deny, when they are in cardiac intensive care, use fewer analgesics. They are in hospital for about one-and-a-half days less than other patients and, on average, back at work faster. The down side is that they're right back into smoking, no exercise, lots of beer and all the things that put them there in the first place, because they deny that those factors have an impact. So denial actually has positive benefits in terms of immediate recovery. Cardiac Intensive Care and Child Burns Units are well-researched areas.

The children in denial have a faster discharge and a faster recovery from their burns. So denial is a very positive strategy in acute situations where there is nothing else you can do.

What about the danger of blaming the victim, the suggestion that if you don't survive, or if you get worse, there is something wrong with your sense of optimism or fighting spirit?

I've talked to a patient who had a very nice insight into that—a very eloquent woman with breast cancer, living in Papua New Guinea with her husband and, of course,

ILLNESS

Papua New Guinea can be a very dangerous place to live these days.

The subject of conversation at a dinner she attended was about a friend who had driven home, got out to pick up some mail at the gate and been mugged. There was much conversation around the dinner table about what he'd done wrong—if he hadn't got out of his car at night to get the mail but waited until the next morning, he wouldn't have been mugged. So that was his mistake. And she said that it was as if, by identifying what he did wrong, we felt secure that it wouldn't happen to us.

And she said that when her mother developed lung cancer she was doing exactly the same thing, saying, 'Well, Mum smoked all her life and even if I've got a lung cancer gene at least I haven't smoked. So that's what Mum did wrong.' And then she said she was appalled to find that when she developed breast cancer, she was getting the same messages from her friends and from the medical staff. It was a subtle way of rewording 'blaming the victim'. But it's not so much blaming the victim as saying, 'If I can identify what you've done to get cancer, then I feel secure because it won't happen to me. I have to see you as different from me.'

So I think that victim blaming may lead us down the wrong path. It's more helpful to think of it in terms of medical staff, nursing staff and friends feeling that they can cope with it because it's not going to happen to them. If we lived in a world where we thought, 'Gosh, this could happen to me too', most of us would find it a fairly frightening world.

9

Ian Hickie

Ian Hickie is Associate Professor of Psychiatry at the University of New South Wales. He is also the Director of the Academic Department of Psychiatry at St George Hospital in Sydney and Convenor of the Australian Behavioural Immunology Group.

What is Psychoimmunology?

Psychoimmunology or Behavioural Immunology is concerned with the relationship between changes in behaviour and changes in the immune system. It is multi-disciplinary and brings together psychiatrists, psychologists, immunologists, veterinarians and laboratory scientists who are interested in the relationships between behaviour, in both animals and humans, immunological processes and illness. So it fundamentally involves collaboration between two groups, one concerned with behaviour and the other with clinical and laboratory immunology.

It is a relatively infant discipline. What is its history in Australia?

The really substantial scientific work in the area has occurred over the last decade. One of the most important and one of the first studies ever in the area was done in Australia by Dr Roger Bartrop, a psychiatrist, and his immunological colleagues at the University of New South Wales. It was the first report of the direct effect of a psychological state on the immune system. The study showed that, after bereavement, people experienced a decline in function of their immune cells.

It looked at people whose spouse had recently died. Immune functions were looked at in the acute bereavement period. What was found was a reduction in the activity and vitality of T-cells, an important component of the immune system. It suggested, for the first time, that there was a direct link between a psychological state—the stressful bereavement state—and a demonstrable change in immune function.

Roger continued to follow those people over time and tried to look at the long-term illness outcome. It was very important work and, once it was replicated in the USA, was taken up by other groups and substantially expanded.

Since that time active research societies in this particular field of psychoimmunology have developed in the USA, Europe and Australia.

There have been many studies which appear to show a link between disease and stress. But there also seem to be a lot of contradictory studies. From the perspective of psychoimmunology, is there a link between stress and disease, is it a causal factor?

Probably the easiest place to start is with the simple animal models. If you create situations of overwhelming stress you will make animals physically sick. A psychological stressor, like overcrowding, will result in disease or illness in laboratory animals. That is, you feed those animals and provide them with all their apparent physical needs, but something about the social situation results in stress ulceration and death.

So, in the animal literature it's clear that there is some kind of relationship between extremely stressful situations and adverse physical health outcomes.

In humans it's obviously a much more complicated situation. We have another kind of problem, because stress is not so easily defined. You can ask about stressful events, but each individual's response to those stressful situations is different. When the stressor is marital separation, difficult children or being exposed to a physiological trauma, not everyone will react in the same way. It's easiest to say that a situation of distress—that is when people become extremely anxious or depressed—is much more clearly linked with poor physical health outcomes. The psychological states of extreme anxiety and extreme depression are clearly linked with immunological changes. Those same states, linked with immune changes and depression, have been shown separately to be linked with physical illness.

If you get very depressed you're going to increase your chances of dying by about a factor of two.

Our state of mind then, can affect our immune system adversely.

The basic questions are: Can the brain normally control the immune system? Can the brain when it is in a changed state, like depression, cause unfavourable changes in the immune system? Further, when the immune system is changed (for example, by infection) can it also change the behaviour of the organism itself?

Research over the last decade has shown two or three of the basic mechanisms by which the brain controls the peripheral immune system. The peripheral immune system consists of the various different types of white blood cells which fight infections and protect us from cancer. The more we find out, the more we show that the brain and the peripheral immune system are intimately connected. That is, they don't behave like two separate systems at all. The brain has a series of very direct ways of regulating peripheral immune function. If there is some threat to the organism, be it psychological or physical, the immune system is part of the coordinated response to that threat.

In terms of your capacity to respond to further threats, it probably matters whether you are already highly distressed. Or if you think of it in terms of recovery, in recuperative terms, then your psychological state is highly likely to influence your capacity to call into action the body's normal mechanism for getting well.

We know in general terms that people's psychological state is one of the most important predictors of recovery from just about any physical illness. If you visit cardiac, respiratory, or gastroenterology wards and you want to know who is going to do badly, you could do a whole range of the physical tests or you could just assess how depressed people are. Depression is a very strong predictor of poor outcome.

Intervening in those states of depression, treating those states, improves recovery. If you talk to patients they'll generally say that what they thought was important in their recovery was something that has a 'psychological ring' to it, in addition to the necessary medical treatment they received. They'll often talk about their own attitudes and the extent to which that influenced the way they dealt with their illness and complied with other aspects of their medical treatment.

How clear is it then that distress affects the immune system?

If you get distressed you do have reduced immune function. The studies we've conducted over the last few years seem to suggest that there is actually a relationship between distress, immune changes and poor physical health outcomes.

There are a lot of factors involved when individuals are faced with a stressful situation. Issues such as: Can I cope? Can I control that situation? Do I feel competent? Or, do I feel overwhelmed? The suggestion is that it is the sense of being overwhelmed that results in distress, anxiety or depression and that's when you do badly. So there are a whole lot of psychological response styles to consider.

Can we see, at times of distress or depression, an actual change in the immune system?

Yes, that's where most of the work is done—in acutely stressful situations. Generally there is a reduction in the performance of the cell-mediated arm of the immune system. The immune system has two broad arms, one has got to do with the production of antibodies (so-called humoral immunity or B-cell dependent arm), the other is the cell-mediated immunity. That T-cell dependent arm is concerned with fighting viral infections and protecting you from cancer.

Now it's that T-cell arm, rather than the B-cell arm, which seems to be most affected by psychological factors.

Most of the experiments in humans and other animals involve exposure to acutely stressful situations. For example, some of the most common studies are done with psychology students in US college programs. Exam stressors or acutely stressful situations are associated with a reduction in certain aspects of cell-mediated immunity or T-cell dependent immunity. The greatest impairment is seen in those people who are most distressed by the situation. The immune system rapidly recovers when the stress passes, so that kind of fluctuation probably isn't so important to the development of illness. It doesn't take much to move your immune system around—it's a very responsive system. If you drink too much, or smoke too much, that will upset your immune system. Sleep deprivation, for example, is another very important factor.

Is it fanciful to imagine that this discipline could be important in preventive medicine?

It is not fanciful. Our premise, based on epidemiological work, is that people of a particular disposition, or type, are more likely than others to develop specific problems.

The general strategy for prevention is to identify high-risk people—high risk either because they've had psychological stress, or high risk because they carry, for example, a genetic risk to a particular disease. That's such hard work to do though. You have to take a large number of people, follow them over a long period of time to see whether something you thought was a good idea was actually worth all the effort.

The shorter-term studies follow smaller cohorts, over a shorter period of time, who are at high-risk—for example, following older persons with depression or following patients with depression in the community. There are some really important studies which generally support the significance of dealing with these psychological issues, not yet across the whole population, but for certain high-risk groups. These studies argue a lot for intervention to prevent bad health outcomes both in terms of suicide outcome and other bad physical health outcomes.

What would be appropriate interventions?

In the depression area, effective treatment in some situations is antidepressants, in other situations non-pharmacological treatments.

A contentious area is studying people who have, for example, a high genetic risk to breast cancer or to bowel cancer. How are we going to assist these people who are at high risk of developing a particular illness? Would psychological intervention be useful in those areas, or would psychological screening be useful? Some of the most interesting outcomes studies that have been done have been in the cancer area, with psychological interventions—group therapies—showing that people who go to these kind of psychological support groups live longer. It's an effective contribution to treatment in addition to the standard medical treatment.

How much longer do they tend to live?

In the breast cancer literature, we're talking about doubling of survival times. There are two issues actually, it's not just the length of survival, it's also the quality of life. The biggest effect is that individuals report that they feel a whole lot better. But beyond feeling a whole lot better they have improved survival times. The most impressive controlled trials have been in breast cancer and melanoma.

That area is called psycho-oncology. Psychological intervention in cancer is developing as a discipline of its own.

It seems to be the opinion of some, even a widespread acceptance, that if people are unhappy, if they are stressed, they are more likely to develop a disease like cancer. How do you respond to this?

There is some evidence to support the notion. Unfortunately, a lot of the evidence is over-interpreted or misinterpreted and becomes, 'It's your fault that you got sick'. We know that's not very helpful at all. What we're talking about is probably a risk factor, a contributing factor in certain situations.

And that's really why high-risk populations are more interesting. If you're already carrying a genetic risk factor or another risk factor to a particular disease, and then you throw in a psychological distress, such as marital breakdown on top of that, it may then be the combination of all three or four factors which really results in developing a particular illness.

Can we move on from the causes or development of a disease or illness to recovery. What do we know about the psychology of recovery?

Evidence in recovery is much stronger than the development of the illness. It's clear that for just about every illness studied, psychological factors have a profound impact on naturalistic recovery. When health care providers have gone in and provided psychological support for those with serious diseases, like a terminal cancer, you get an improvement in survival. So I think that the notion that psychological functioning is critical to recovery has been demonstrated in a lot of different areas.

How close are we to concluding then that our psychology and its effect on the immune system is vital to recovery?

Studies of these particular types are difficult to do, but in a sense I think they affirm the belief that people have that they need to take account of the wider context in which illness happens. Medicine hasn't always been preoccupied with reducing disability, sometimes it's more preoccupied with cure and with the simplest kind of medical management.

So the research is difficult to do in different areas, and working out all the bits that are important and how they fit together is quite complicated. We don't think it's going to be very simple. We can't say, if we do 'this' the immune system changes and people will get better. It's likely to be much more complex than that.

But the work has the capacity to educate us and the people we work with as to which factors are most important and contribute most to the best functional outcomes, the greatest degree of recovery.

10

Simon Champ

In his teenage years when he was still at school, Simon suffered what was thought to be a nervous breakdown. Not long after, he was diagnosed with schizophrenia.

During breaks in our first long conversation at his house, I studied some of his paintings. He is a gifted artist and poet which told me something of the man who, during our time together, drew me into the world of his childhood, the terror of the disease and the courageous battle he has fought to conquer the illness.

ILLNESS

Simon, what do you remember most about your childhood?

Well, my father was in the British Air Force, so we travelled all the time, and lived in other countries. I lived in Israel and Aden for a number of years, although I was actually born in France. And I was a bit of a loner in some ways. I was always the new kid on the school block. I came to Australia to live when I was fourteen.

Can you tell me a bit more about your younger life, your family life . . . do you have siblings?

I've got two brothers, one of them is fourteen years younger than me and the other, two years younger. I don't remember a lot about my childhood in many ways. I think it's interesting that I very much see my life before and after the psychosis—after becoming mentally ill. I think I was a happy child. I was overweight and teased a lot by other kids, which didn't help, but within myself I was reasonably content. I loved animals and birds and I loved drawing.

I did reasonably well at school even though I moved school every two to three years. And before I got sick I was trying to decide what I was going to do with my life, like every teenager, and I was torn between my fascination with zoology, animals and birds, and my interest in art. Somebody recently asked me, 'What did you really want to be when you were young?', and in a way I realised that I'd never really had a chance to form myself because schizophrenia came on when I was seventeen, although it wasn't diagnosed as such. People just said I'd had a nervous breakdown.

Although you went to many different schools, did you have opportunities to make friendships?

Yes, particularly when I was at school in Israel, I had a lot of friends there. It was an international school and it's the school that sticks in my memory out of all the places I went to.

My father was in the Diplomatic Corps at that stage and because the school was an international school kids from many countries went there. I think it was a very exciting time just living in Israel. It was just after the 1967 war and we did a lot of exploration of the country, visited all the holy sites. So for me it was a very rich time. I didn't understand the politics of the Middle East but the curiosity of a thirteen-year-old just kept me going. It was fascinating. And my school friends . . . I guess it was the closest I had to a period where life was fairly normal in terms of schooling.

Was there a particular friend you remember from your childhood who was hard to say good-bye to?

Gee! Probably my friends at the school in Israel. It's interesting, I can remember the whole class there, and it's the only place where I can remember all the kids. Sometimes I wonder whether I shut down to cope with so much travel, whether perhaps I handled separation differently from other people.

What do you mean by that?

Well, I just wonder about the affect on a kid of constantly saying goodbye to people. Whether you become more ambivalent about friendships. I think I'm very loyal to my friends, so maybe I compensate in other ways, and perhaps I try now to maintain my friendships with an intensity that I didn't have as a child.

Were you ever apprehensive about packing up and moving off again as a child?

I think it must have been very hard to have to pack up every two years and suddenly lose your friends and not know whether you would see them again. It must have been very hard, and one of the things I've felt over the last few years is that I don't have a sense of communities growing up together, or long-term friendships. Even when

ILLNESS

I came to Australia I travelled a lot with my parents and so that pattern of staying in one place for only a few years continued for quite a while. Now I've lived in Sydney for nearly fifteen years. I've moved a lot during that time but Sydney has been my base so I've got friends I have had for quite a while and that's been a big help in terms of my illness—having friends who know me well.

Do you have other childhood memories of the things that were important to you?

A lot of the time I remember going for walks and looking at animals and birds, that was my big passion—particularly bird-watching—and it was fairly solitary. For a number of years I kept drawing animals and birds. I was just fascinated by them. The fascination has diminished as I've gotten older. But, I think with birds it was their ability to fly—it was beautiful. I'd study their eggs and their nests and knew all their names and I could identify just about any bird in any country where I lived.

Did your family share the same interests?

Not really, but they were supportive of my interests, my interest in art—there wasn't art in the family although my brother has grown up to be a sculptor in Adelaide. We went through art school together at one stage. When I was in my teenage years, art became very important to me and I became very involved with painting and drawing.

Over the last few years I've become interested in classical music—a great sort of balm for the soul. I find that, as part of my recovery or living with schizophrenia, there are a lot of emotions to work through and I find that music helps me as a kind of therapy. It releases a lot of emotions that I struggle with when I'm sick and when I'm trying to come to terms with my schizophrenia.

As a child you loved birds and animals, did you have a pet of your own?

I had a dog at one place I lived but I had to give him up after about a year and it broke my heart. I was always collecting animals of one kind or another, but I had to give up my pets.

I'd find wild animals and birds which were sick and look after them. In one place I lived I had a marvellous collection of frogs and toads in a big box. When I came to Australia my mother was horrified when she discovered that I kept scorpions I'd found in an aquarium. We lived on a farm at the time. I had a very young brother and she thought it was really dangerous for him, but I was the keen naturalist fascinated by keeping these scorpions. I remember I kept them in my bedroom.

Can you tell me about your early experiences when you first arrived in Australia?

We came first of all to South Australia where Dad was selling lemonade for a while—he was a salesman for a lemonade company. He started a new life, basically. And then he got a job as manager of an Aboriginal reserve in South Australia so we went to this very remote place, Point McLeay Aboriginal Reserve, and spent a year there.

Do you remember much about that Reserve?

Yes, I remember reverse prejudice. I didn't understand the politics of Aboriginal culture at that stage—this was about 1971 or 1972—so I'd travel to school and be one of the few white kids on a bus full of Aboriginals. And we were the ones who were the victims of racism in a sense. We were the minority, so there were a lot of taunts—you know, 'You white . . . "swear words" . . .', just a lot of racism about the fact that we were white. I don't like the thought of the politics of Reserves now but at that stage I didn't understand. And it was very sad in many ways because what had been a Mission was now a Reserve and there wasn't the pride in Aboriginal culture that there is now. My mother used to call it, 'The prettiest ghetto on earth'.

What are your thoughts about those sorts of Reserves now?
I'm very interested in Aboriginal culture, and my interest in Aboriginal Art has led me to an awareness of Aboriginal culture which I didn't have back then. There's a lot to learn from Aboriginal culture.

I've always been fascinated by Northern American Indian culture—particularly the relationship to the land and spirituality—and I also find a lot of wisdom in Aboriginal culture.

I'm involved in mental health policy—I'm an adviser to the Federal Minister on mental health issues through a group I'm involved in called The National Community Advisory Group—and one of the issues that is raised is Aboriginal mental health. It's a very specialised area but the damage to Aboriginal culture has affected the mental health of the Aboriginal people very severely.

I don't think you can look at Aboriginal mental health without actually taking into account the history of cultural displacement and the cultural grieving of Aboriginal peoples. As a white person I feel I shouldn't be involved in it, but the area of Aboriginal mental health has distinctly different issues to any other of mental health, and that's because separation of children from their families and things like that have led to complications in their mental health. And I believe there's an element of grieving in Aboriginal populations that actually has an effect on the rate of depression.

After that year on the Reserve, where did you move next?
For a while we lived in Meningie—we lived on the Coorong for two years renting a farmhouse when Dad was managing a hospital in town. Again, it was a very isolated period for me because we were living fourteen miles out of town, and I lived a life like the boy in Colin

Thiele's book *Storm Boy*. I could really identify with that story because I spent a lot of time on my own just walking through the paddocks and sand-hills watching the pelicans and spending endless hours studying the birds and insects.

I was doing a lot of drawing at that point in my life. Then we moved to Mt Gambier, and it was at that time that I was doing my HSC and had my first nervous breakdown. My father was managing a retirement village there, and that was really the beginning of the change in my life. I was seventeen.

There were my trial exams, and that might've been the pressure that triggered the first breakdown. Schizophrenia seems to need some kind of a trigger to set it off. For many people it's actually drug use that can trigger the first episode but I'd never used drugs and all of a sudden I was having these experiences that were very similar to drug-induced experiences. When I tried to understand what had happened to me I started reading literature and . . . God, it takes me back.

Do you feel like talking about that period?
Yes, this is very interesting. I haven't been asked these questions before. I wonder if I've actually forgotten a lot of my life. Anyway, I had a breakdown when I was seventeen and then I was all right until my early twenties.

When you say breakdown, what does that mean? Were you hospitalised?
No, I wasn't hospitalised. I heard things on the radio that weren't there, I acted very strangely at school and was out of touch with reality.

What did your parents do at that stage? Did they take you to a doctor?
They took me to a doctor eventually but they weren't sure what was happening. They'd thought that maybe I'd taken drugs or that somebody had given me drugs.

Were you put on medication at that stage?

No, and at that time it wasn't diagnosed as schizophrenia. I left school and went and worked in the forest for a few months as a labourer and then I went back and finished my HSC the next year. Then I went to art school in Adelaide, but didn't finish my studies. I was always dropping out and was very strange during those times, because a lot of the time I was suffering from paranoia and the beginnings of schizophrenia without realising what I was dealing with. I was in my early twenties when I got really sick. At one stage I hitchhiked up the east coast and was living in Byron Bay. Then I started getting really strange and I had my first major psychotic breakdown.

Were you taking drugs up in Byron Bay?

No. I'd had some when I was at art school but I wasn't a heavy drug user at all. And I wasn't taking anything in Byron Bay. But I was becoming more and more withdrawn, living by myself and getting stranger and stranger.

I was told that I had schizophrenia after those breakdowns and at first I was almost relieved that I knew what was happening to me, but then I started reading books on schizophrenia to understand what was happening, and I got very depressed because it was all so negative.

After one of my breakdowns I think I made a conscious decision that I would live life as an experiment, because the stuff that I was reading about schizophrenia was so negative. If I believed that, life wasn't worth living. So I tried to find a way of redefining schizophrenia for myself. And that's a process that I've been involved with for the last fifteen years, with other people with schizophrenia, trying to find out what works for us in our lives and trying to build a better sense of what's achievable with an illness like schizophrenia. I find that I look at young people with the illness, and their sense of potential of life is better than for my generation of people—those of us who were diagnosed with schizophrenia fifteen years ago or more. I don't think it's any easier to live with the illness than it was, but there is less stigma and there is more support for people. I've been one of the people involved in fighting for a change along that line.

There's a recurring nature to the schizophrenia that I've got so I get sick usually about once every fifteen months, and I can sometimes get depressed about that—that it's going to come again.

What do we know about schizophrenia and how is it best managed?

People talk about schizophrenia, but really we should talk about 'schizophrenias'. There are a whole range of illnesses under that label, and I don't think we know really what those illnesses are at the moment. There still needs to be so much more research. We don't know the causes, we don't know what form the different illnesses can take.

For example, I'm very lucky in that I don't usually hear voices in my head and I don't usually hallucinate, but I get awful paranoid delusions and think that people are trying to poison me and a world government is trying to exterminate the unemployed and all kinds of weird ideas like that. And when they're happening it really makes life fairly impossible for me and very frightening.

But, I do go into remission and for most of the time I'm fine and I'm able to function well. I live on a pension still but I supplement my income with part-time work on various committees and giving talks about the illness. But as much as I've recovered or learnt to manage the illness—I think that's a better way of putting it—I still seem to need a lot of time to myself to be able to do that. I would find it very hard to work a nine-to-five job. Some people manage it with schizophrenia, but I can't.

Managing your illness means what?

It means monitoring stress levels in my life quite a bit. I'm tied to taking medication, and that helps, but it's also about watching the change in your emotional life because that can trigger another episode. That doesn't mean to say that you have to live a flat, dull life, but you should just be aware of pressures in life which might be more stressful than normal.

Was there an intervention at a particular time that helped you most?

I think the first thing that helped me was that after I was first hospitalised with schizophrenia I was given a chance to go to a therapeutic community—a halfway house run by the Richmond Fellowship. I spent a year living in this house where there were six men and six women at any one time, at different stages of recovery from their psychiatric illnesses. Most of them were either schizophrenic or had a manic depressive illness. What happened there was that I got some sense of hope, and I can't overestimate the value of hope.

I saw other people with schizophrenia getting on with their lives—getting back to the work force or getting back into study or back into relationships, and there was some sense that my life wouldn't always be lying in a beanbag feeling very depressed and feeling that my life was over, because that's what I felt when I was in hospital, that life was really over for me.

I do a lot of work now talking to younger people with schizophrenia and trying to instil that hope because I think that the suicide rate amongst people with schizophrenia is about 15 per cent within the first five years of their diagnosis. My belief is that that high suicide rate is linked to despair and hopelessness and stigma.

People don't commit suicide because they're psychotic and acting out some fantasy, they do it because they've internalised stigma and they feel hopeless about their lives. Those things can be changed, and the suicide rate could come down. But it's a battle; the illness does make you feel so hopeless sometimes.

Tell me a bit more about your time in that shared house, did you do things together—was the group compatible?

It was an incredible experience. We were people from all walks of life and backgrounds and really the only thing we had in common was the fact that we'd all had a psychiatric diagnosis. And we'd encourage each other. It was like living in a very big and complex share-house, with the addition that some of us were very sick people sometimes. We received a lot of counselling there about our illnesses and about what our medications did, which was important because fifteen years ago, and even now, a lot of people don't get any basic information about why they need medication. And then they wonder why people are non-compliant!

So you had a sense of optimism and hope at that point?

Yes. It would fluctuate, but it was the beginning of a sense that life could get better for me.

And that there was a way of living again?

Yes. I didn't know how to. In those early years I was getting sick every three months; life was a constant juggling of high levels of medication and sometimes I'd drink quite a bit to deal with my feelings. It was constant juggling and never knowing whether I'd be well the next day. When I look back at that period it was very hard.

Do you think that the psychiatric profession has always dealt with you appropriately?

I was relatively lucky. I think that all too often the profession sees medication as being the only answer for people with schizophrenia. My feeling is that medication only stabilises. And to come good with schizophrenia, you really need a lot of counselling and support.

And did you get that?

I started to get it, but in a way I created it for myself. I was involved in the establishment of the Schizophrenia Fellowship of New South Wales in 1985. That was really the first time that people with schizophrenia had come together to try to lobby and meet each other, and that was important for me.

So you became politicised at that stage?

Yes, mainly because the house I was living in offered support but what I saw around me were so many people who weren't getting support: the vast majority of people with schizophrenia were getting no support at all, and I was just outraged. And also the things that were said about people with schizophrenia, the negative stereotypes. Around that time there was an article headed 'The Illness That Breeds Killers'. We were supposed to be axe-murderers according to the popular press, and it was very hard to live with that level of stigma. And still is. It's improved a little but still the vast majority of people are afraid and suspicious of people with schizophrenia.

How did you become involved in setting up the Schizophrenia Fellowship?

It came together out of a group of us who were wanting to see more lobbying and support for people with schizophrenia. It's grown into quite a big organisation now but, essentially, in the beginning it was just a series of meetings in about nine different locations in Sydney. People would meet and share their experiences and we'd try to get speakers to talk about medication or services.

For me one of the really important things was that people with schizophrenia began to socialise together and meet and talk about what worked in our lives. Around about that time there was also a group of people with schizophrenia I became involved with, set up by a psychiatrist and who met every Monday night for about eight years. And that was very important because we've supported each other through our lives.

An illness like schizophrenia affects your whole life. It affects the way you relate to people, the way that you live your life, how you work, how you live day-to-day. A lot of your life and lifestyle gets disrupted and I think sometimes only people with schizophrenia know what it's like. A lot of my support has come from other people with schizophrenia.

Outside your political involvement what have been your other activities?

I finished my degree at Sydney College of the Arts, and did postgraduate studies there in painting. It was good because I found myself mixing with people who had never heard of schizophrenia and, up until then, since I'd been sick, most of my friends had been other people with schizophrenia or professionals in the area. And I found I was able to broaden my interests. Also, because I started appearing in the media and lobbying about schizophrenia, a lot of the people at college actually became very strong supporters—encouraging me in my political work as an activist. And feeding back to me how they perceived what I was doing and the value of what I was doing, which was very important. It was interesting because sometimes I'd be angry about the way people with schizophrenia were treated and I'd think it was just because I had schizophrenia, but my friends at college would actually say, 'No, you're right, what is happening to people with schizophrenia is outrageous'. And when other people saw it that way, I knew I was onto something.

I think a large part of my recovery has actually depended on my paintings and keeping diaries, although I'm not painting at the moment, but for a number of years I was able to work out a lot of my feelings that way. At that time I did paintings and drawings about the history of psychiatry and through that I was able to work out my feelings about being part of a stigmatised minority in society.

And also very emotional stuff. There were times when it was really hard to live with schizophrenia and, in one way or another painting, drawing and writing helped me to work through those emotions. I could take a fairly therapeutic approach in my work and still get recognition for my skills. It was a good course.

What sort of postgraduate work did you do?

Part of what I looked at was the experience of Shamans in different cultures, and the initiatory experience of Shamans, how their vision quests often look like psychotic material if you read it out of context. How they can manage to reintegrate that kind of up-welling from the unconscious when people with schizophrenia can't, fascinated me.

The Shaman is the medicine man or woman of the tribe, a kind of witch doctor figure, the healer. In different cultures Shamans are chosen and go through initiations, and very often during that process they have visions induced—either through the use of drugs, or through isolation or physical kinds of tasks.

When you read, out of context, accounts of those visions and what happens to them when they are in those altered states, it reads a lot like a schizophrenic experience. But they have control over it and can move in and out of those states at will, whereas a person with schizophrenia, once they are in a psychotic state, can only be helped by medication.

Since the 1980s, particularly when schizophrenia was seen as a biochemical imbalance in the brain, there's been very little attention paid to the actual phenomena of what's actually manifesting, or the content of peoples' delusions.

Sometimes I believe that when you have a psychotic

attack, it's like dreaming. Perhaps there's material in there which may be useful. Perhaps there are messages from our unconscious in psychosis which need to be integrated into our lives. But the medical profession says that's invalid. I'm not sure. A lot of it I'd prefer not to live through, anyway.

Through my poetry and writings I've tried to understand it in some way because, with schizophrenia, it feels as if so much of your time is wasted by this illness. If it's got no meaning, then it's a waste of time, and no-one wants to believe that.

What happened to your painting at postgraduate level, did you do much more then?

Yes, I was painting a lot and then the last year I stopped, and I don't know why. I had a one-man show of paintings and drawings at the Performance Space Gallery. At the time there was a documentary film being made about schizophrenia and I was one of the people featured, so the exhibition was part of the documentary.

I was very pleased with it. Everything about people with schizophrenia is stereotyped, even their art. There's this belief that people with mental illness paint in a certain way. It's perceived as outsider art. I think I consciously set out to show a range of my art to redress that problem of stereotyping. For example, in the exhibition there were very realistic drawings of animals I'd done at the zoo, there were very abstract works and there were very metaphorical works with a spiritual interest in them.

When I first met you, you talked about recovery and explained that schizophrenia has really three distinct categories, can you elaborate on that?

People talk about the rule of thirds in schizophrenia. I don't know that I agree with it, but the theory is that some people will only have one or two breakdowns and then they will recover completely; other people are like me and they will have recurring episodes throughout their lives; and some people will never get well at all, never actually come out of the psychosis. I think that's changing a little bit now because there are better medications.

There's also a range of illnesses and degrees of disability that people experience because of their illnesses, and for me what it means is that, because I have recurrent episodes, I maximise the times when I'm in remission to try to improve my life. But I'm living with the sense that I probably will get sick again at some time in the future.

Recovery is like an ongoing process for some people with schizophrenia in that you're constantly recovering. Some people do get well, some people never have another episode after they've had one or two. I've got friends like that and I sometimes think, 'Why can't that happen for me? Why do I have to go through episode after episode after episode?' I take good care of myself and I do all the right things according to medication, but I still get sick periodically.

You said that the episodes occur approximately every 15 months. Between episodes what sort of life do you lead?

At the moment I do a lot of lecturing about schizophrenia and mental health issues. I'm on the National Community Advisory Group on mental health issues, which is a body that advises the Federal Government and the Health Minister on the implementation of the strategic plan in mental health. So a lot of my time is involved in lobbying and supporting other people with schizophrenia.

I spend time painting and writing and I do a lot of reading. I find that I'm always reading. I think that helps me find new ways of presenting material and new ideas. I like to visit friends and I still spend quite a bit of time on my own. I seem to need that, although sometimes it can be lonely as well.

I'm discovering that there's such a thing as the mid-life crisis and I think I'm having a major one. It's slightly different for people with schizophrenia because, in my early twenties, so much of what I would like to have done I couldn't do because I was sick. And so over recent years I've actually had a lot of firsts—I went overseas and I went to a conference in Ireland to deliver a paper on Human Rights. All these things I did for the first time.

And as I am approaching forty, life is becoming an unknown rather than a known. For a lot of people life becomes a known quantity as they reach their middle years, whereas I'm functioning better than I've ever functioned before so, there's a sense of beginning things.

In terms of ambition I don't know what my potential is with this illness. I'm staying well longer and consolidating my wellness has allowed me to do things that I've never done before. In a broad sense it's about maximising my potential. I'd like to still have some influence in terms of how people saw schizophrenia, and perhaps write something about it because I give a lot of lectures, but I don't actually get a lot down on paper.

Do you see yourself as an artist?
At the moment I am not sure that I do. I think that if I am going to be involved in art it has to change for me, because it seems the empowering device for my art was actually a kind of therapeutic relationship with it, rather than wanting to be an artist as such. I painted out of a need for therapy, I think.

Would your teachers have said that you were talented?
Oh, yes, they did. But I feel there's only so much you can do with painting. And as far as influencing the way that people see schizophrenia, there are other more effective ways. I pick up a brush occasionally and get a thrill out of it, but I can't see where my painting is going. My diaries, on the other hand, interest me and I keep writing. There's an interest in unravelling the self, understanding myself. One of the things that's hard for me is that most

of my adult life was affected so much by schizophrenia, and I'm seeing that life experience is not just schizophrenia anymore.

Because of that there are new problems to solve. In a sense I don't have the excuse of schizophrenia any more, and now at forty I'm wanting to discover what it was like to be twenty-five or thirty, because at those times I missed out on certain things.

The problem is choice rather than limitation. And there's a fresh sense of grieving sometimes—for the life that I've lost because of schizophrenia. I think also there's a sense of the business of life being what you *do*. And that's a hard one for me. With an illness like schizophrenia you're forced to confront the meaning of life or question what you're doing in life more than perhaps most people. Because for long periods you're out of work, you're forced to find an identity that isn't dependent on work, or find meaning from things other than work. And also, because you're out of touch with reality when you're sick, you question the nature of reality—something most people don't really have to do.

That's why I enjoy the friendships I have with people with schizophrenia because there's a depth to them—their search for meaning, because of their illnesses, is usually a very deep one.

You spoke earlier of a spiritual life. Are you a religious person?

No, I'm not. One of the things I learned when I was diagnosed with schizophrenia, was that there is a lot of prejudice within the churches. I found religious people quite commonly had the idea that you must have sinned to get schizophrenia or that you were possessed in some way.

I was deeply hurt and wounded by that kind of thinking. I tried very hard at one stage to become a Christian, but over the years I've looked more at Zen, Buddhism, Eastern religions and taken from many religions—a little wisdom from each one. Nature itself nourishes me, too. And living in the city I don't seem to get that in the same way I did when I've lived for periods by the ocean.

What attracts you to the Buddhist philosophy?

In Buddhism there's a lot about not attaching oneself to sorrow. If you've got schizophrenia you've got a lot of sorrow and Buddhism teaches ways of not letting that hold you back, not getting attached to the sorrow. There was a period where I knew a lot of people with schizophrenia and, as a consequence, I knew a lot of people who suicided as well, and it really wore me down.

What is the most important thing you have to say to young people with schizophrenia?

Don't give up. It sounds simplistic, but you don't know what life with an illness like schizophrenia holds for you. You don't know what your potential is, you've got to find it. And don't believe the negative literature, stereotyping and the stigma. Find your own reality with the illness. Unfortunately, that is a slow process. It's very hard for a young person to say that in five years time they'll be better or more able to manage the illness.

It's important to allow yourself to feel the emotions: to work through the grief, the anger and denial—all the stages you go through; to say, 'I'm angry because I've got this illness', and work through those feelings, share them with others. Also the sadness of being a person with schizophrenia: for many people it does make our lives incredibly lonely at times. It's important to acknowledge those things so that your healing takes place faster.

Another important thing is that there are role models, other people with schizophrenia, to talk to who have been living with the illness longer. Talk to them about how they live with their illness, practical things about how they deal with their medication, their symptoms and the voices or delusions. Part of this coming out of people with mental illness is that there is a body of knowledge and wisdom that's been compiled about the illness from a first-hand experience. So tap into that and make use of friendships with other people with schizophrenia.

And what would you say to people who discriminate against those with schizophrenia?

I'd say, give people a go with schizophrenia. They have far more potential than they're usually given credit for. In employment, for example, people with schizophrenia can make good workers, but they don't get the opportunities because people are afraid of us. And we don't need to be locked up and put out of sight. They're often very sensitive and feeling people.

It's up to us as well to not exist under the shadow of shame. I feel that for fifteen years I've been battling the image of people with schizophrenia and trying to present a more positive one. It's been hard but worth it because we couldn't live the way people used to see us. It was too lonely.

I feel that there's a lot more hope in life than I envisaged when I was younger. Generally, life gets better as I get older. There are setbacks along the way, but I have an ability to live life in a deeper way as I get older. And a freer way—freer from the schizophrenia.

More joy perhaps?

Yes, and there is a sense of an appreciation of things. A joy in freedom from hardship. To have suffered from schizophrenia makes you appreciate the good times more.

I look at life as very much a journey and my journey has been entwined with learning to live with schizophrenia and overcome it. As I get older that's become less a part of my journey. I've learnt to manage the illness so it's not a daily struggle any more. It gives me more energy, I'm free to live life more fully, and that gives me a lot more hope for the future.

And, as I say, at this stage of my life there are a lot more firsts. Like when I went to Ireland and spoke at a conference. Twenty years ago I could never have imagined that. When the illness began I felt that my life was over, literally. I felt I could never achieve anything. There were times when I wondered if it was worthwhile living. I don't have that problem any more.

11

Rosemary Lorz

In the course of research for this book I was invited along to a support group for people with mental illness to meet the group's convenor, Elizabeth Field, and some participants. When Rosemary, a friendly, outgoing young woman, approached me to introduce herself, I assumed she was someone helping to run the group. But I was to discover that, like Simon Champ, she too has battled schizophrenia.

Subsequently I visited Rosemary and her mother at their home. They displayed an immense generosity and openness in relating their deeply emotional personal stories. We shared laughter and tears but, above all, their stories gave me hope for other young people who experience the illness.

ROSEMARY LORZ

Can you tell me about your early life?

For the first five years of my life I was very happy, very outgoing. Even my parents said how outgoing I was, but when I started school at the age of five, things weren't really the same. My school teachers used to say, 'Rosemary lives in her own world'. It may have started then, I don't know. As a child I was actually never really happy. I could sense there was something wrong.

But a lot of kids are shy. Do you think it was shyness?

It could have been just shyness. But as I said, I was an average happy child until I was about five years old. I used to go and play with my friends next door. The usual things. I used to play trains with the boy next door and I was into fairly active games. The neighbours had a jeep out in their backyard and we used to play in that. And I played at another girl's house. I just wanted to play every day with my friends really.

And you felt happy?

Yes, I was really happy. I felt there was nothing wrong. But then at the age of five we moved to Carlingford. We used to live in Chester Hill at that time and that was a more multicultural place. But when we moved, everything was of a higher standard and the neighbours used to say, 'Oh, those foreigners!'. It was a very different experience.

Tell me what your background is. Where are your parents from?

They weren't born in Australia. My father is German and my mother is Austrian. Our neighbours were all Australian and I think that was a problem. I felt I was under pressure from them when we moved house.

There was a teacher next door who seemed to keep an eye on me and what I used to do and say. And then there was someone else across the road who used to say, 'Oh, I think Rosemary has slipped with her language', because she was always telling me, 'Don't say "yeah", say "yes" '. She kept correcting me.

Do you think there was a problem with your neighbours because your parents were migrants?

Yes, I think so.

So you started to feel different?

Yes, I did. And at the age of eight I had problems at school. The teacher said the only thing I was good at was sport. And I *was* good at sport but that was probably because I liked athletics and swimming. And in primary school, it was probably my strongest point at that time. I really loved sport.

What about Maths, English and History?

I wasn't very good at those subjects but I was good at singing. I was in the school choir. I enjoyed that. But I wasn't very good at other academic subjects. I was fairly average—sort of on the borderline. And then at the age of eight my father tried to teach me subjects like Maths and I just didn't understand it. I could have done a lot better in high school too. I got a lot of grade threes.

What was your relationship like with your parents?

When I was older I resented the way my mother treated me. I remember when I used to play kids' games with my father and my mother would suddenly hit me—just hit me. That used to really hurt. She never got angry at my father because she knew that he would get even angrier, so she took it out on me. And I used to always spill things because I just wasn't very well balanced.

Were you nervous?

Yes, and a bit unbalanced too. I remember my mother got so angry at one stage she threw everything off the table. She was just really bad with her nerves, and I had a funny relationship with my father, really. He wasn't like the father he should have been. He could have been more encouraging.

So when you were a young child your relationship with your parents was difficult.

It was very hard. And my mother never got along with my grandmother—her mother-in-law. I always seemed to be in the middle of their arguments. My mother would want me to take her side and my grandmother did the same thing. I was torn between them. It was like a triangle. Very stressful. And there were times when my father said, 'I'm leaving. I'm not coming back'. And my mother would be crying and saying that he should come back and I'd be hearing all this and it made me feel very insecure. As I got older there was always something. The stress never seemed to go away.

You think tension in the family made things worse.

Yes, I think so. I didn't really have a proper relationship with my mother. I didn't have the tender loving care from her and I missed all that. But it's part of growing I suppose.

And there was stress at school.

Yes, that too. I had an American friend when I was in high school who had a bit of a reputation because she smoked and was interested in boys. I was influenced by her, I suppose, so the schoolteachers used to think I was bad too. But then she left in Year 9 and went back to America. After she left I had a very hard time making friends again. I didn't have anybody. And I didn't really want to leave school because I didn't know what I wanted to do. So I kept going until Years 11 and 12. Year 11 was OK, but I failed in Year 12.

After that I did a course at a Receptionist Centre and from there you're supposed to be able to get a job, but I never did. I went to about twenty interviews but I didn't get a job.

Then someone told me about another business college, so I went there. I saw the woman in charge and I just burst into tears. I told her I couldn't find a job. She was very helpful because she had a daughter who had schizophrenia too. But at that time I didn't know I had schizophrenia. She was an older lady and very patient. I became accurate with my typing but I had problems with shorthand—I found that hard. But I did a test at the Public Service and passed it so I got a job at Sydney Tech as a typist there.

How old were you then?

I was nineteen when I started working at Sydney Tech. I worked in the counselling unit which I found very hard because I didn't feel I could relate to anybody there. They were psychologists and I found it a strange environment. I just got more and more depressed, and the counsellors didn't help me because nobody knew what was wrong. I was there for five years.

Did you make friends there?

Not really, no. That's when I first started hearing voices and having strange feelings. I got more and more stressed out. I was about twenty-four years old by then.

It was quite bad, but I thought it was kind of special as well. I felt good when I was hearing these voices because I used to imagine that it was the boss at work talking to me. I felt as if I was her child and she was telling me what to do.

In a helpful way?

Yes. The voice was always directing me saying, 'It's your father, it's your father'. The voice was telling me that he was the problem. I used to think, 'What can I do about it?' But I knew there was something wrong and the voice was an indication.

What happened then?

I was told to go on sick leave, so I was gone for six weeks. I went away with my parents up to the Whitsundays for a week.

Did you see a doctor at all?

Oh yes. I went to a doctor—a psychiatrist—and I told her I was feeling depressed and so she put me on Tofrinil, but that didn't really help. She'd given me Tofrinil when I first went to see her when I was twenty-one.

Why were you given Tofrinil?

I was working in the counselling unit and by then I was starting to feel depressed. My mother said, 'Why don't you go and see my psychiatrist?' She was seeing her as well. But antidepressants didn't really help me at that time. Tofrinil is an antidepressant. I had a blood test and was told I was anaemic too, so I needed iron.

So I went back to the same psychiatrist and I told her that Tofrinil wasn't doing me any good. In fact I got much worse. I started getting palpitations. I told her that I was hearing voices. Then she put me on Largactil and soon after that she increased the dose, so I was like a zombie, I couldn't do anything. And my parents couldn't understand why I was sleeping so long. They got very angry because I went to bed all the time.

Did it help with the voice?

Finally, after six months, it went away. The psychiatrist didn't want to put me into a hospital because she thought I should be looked after at home. So, eventually those voices went, but I had funny feelings. I felt the psychiatrist was touching me, which was strange. But that all went away too.

ILLNESS

Were you hearing a number of voices?

When I was really bad I heard other voices. They were people from my work. It was getting out of control so that's when I had to leave and saw the psychiatrist. She told me then that I had schizophrenia. That was really quite awful, because she had to try to explain it to my father as well. And it took him a long time to understand because we'd never heard of it before, never heard of such a thing.

How did your mother and father react to this news?

They were quite upset about it really, and didn't know what to do. They were scared.

Did you talk to them about it?

Well, I didn't know much about it myself. And because of the medication I got to a point where one night we were eating together and I got lockjaw—I couldn't chew and I wasn't able to eat or speak. I went and lay down on the sofa and my mother rang the doctor who prescribed a relaxant and that seemed to help. The next day everything seemed to be a lot better, but I still had side-effects.

When I took out all the tablets I was taking my father said, 'Oh, my God! Do you have to take all of them? I hope you don't become addicted.' But the doctor said they weren't addictive. Yes, my family took it very badly. My sister tried to help, too. She wanted me to try to get into a program that might help me and she found out about a special program for young people.

I went there with my mother and they interviewed me about what I'd been through. Then a week later they said I could start. I found that there were other people there with mental illness and thought, 'Oh, there are others who are just like me', and I felt relieved.

So before that, you'd felt you were the only person in the world with this problem.

Yes, and my parents felt that too because they'd never heard of it before. When it first started they thought that I would grow out of it, but it just got worse. I found the Young Peoples' Program really helped me. There was a lot of psychotherapy where you could talk about your problems, and we had art therapy. I used to like all that sort of thing—games and cooking and you could go on outings. They had camps which was really good because I found the people there were very friendly and helpful. I was there for six months and by then they said that I'd improved quite a lot, so I had to leave the full-time program. But I'd been an in-patient for six months by then.

And what was the daily routine there?

It was like a school, really. In the morning they had social skills and cooking and then there was art therapy, psycho-education and sometimes we did clerical work—we learnt how to write business letters and such things. That was useful.

Was it a problem for you being away from home?

No, I liked it very much. I really enjoyed it.

Did you make friends there?

Yes I did, and some of them I still know now. Every year I went on their camps and I used to enjoy that. Later on I went to the outpatient group meetings once a month, and that was very helpful too. When I was at YPP I found a voluntary job a couple of days a week and then I got paid work out of that.

What was the job?

It was secretarial work. That was one day a week to begin with, but then it increased to two days a week. It was a one-year contract so I did it for a year, then I went back to voluntary work for a couple of years mainly because I'd had a horse-riding accident on a camp in 1991 and injured my leg.

What sort of voluntary work did you do then?

It was always secretarial. I did a couple of years of that and then I went to the Commonwealth Rehabilitation Service. And at that time, at the Schizophrenia Fellowship, I spoke to someone about the work that was going on at Rozelle Hospital. It was consumer consultant's work. I did the training program, and halfway through 1994 I got the job there.

Can you tell me about the work of a consumer consultant and what it entails?

I visit the patients at Rozelle Hospital, in the acute wards and the cottages, and I talk to them about anything they want to talk about. I explain to them that I've had schizophrenia and share my experiences with them. If they've got any complaints, we can take them back to our supervisor. We work in pairs, which is really good. I've always liked the job.

How long have you been doing that?

Over a year now. But in the beginning I found it quite hard to continue and I got to the point where I wanted to resign.

Was it hard working with patients with schizophrenia when you were on the road to recovery yourself?

Yes, it was. I found it very difficult. That was why I wanted to leave in the beginning. It was very hard seeing all those strange people and the way they were. I thought, 'Oh, I've been through this I don't want to see it again'. But the group therapy made me a bit stronger—one with

Elizabeth Field. I found it helped me keep going. And I also needed to work out problems with my father.

So, at that stage you were working as a consumer consultant, but you still felt that you had unresolved problems with your father and you wanted to talk to somebody about it.

Yes, that's right. I never ever really could, and my mother couldn't either. We needed help. Even when we went to psychiatrists, they didn't seem to understand, which was really strange. We talked to my psychiatrist and she'd say, 'You can't change people'. It was very lucky to have someone like Elizabeth to talk to, because she seemed to really understand—it was as if she'd been through it herself.

Tell me about Elizabeth Field. How did you meet her?

She had been helping us through the training course for the consumers job—she did the stress management. Then she started this group called TEAM. They call it 'accelerated learning'. We had meditation and relaxation. A lot of it is self-expression—how to express yourself and speak in public. And to *be* somebody really. It came to a point where my parents even went to see Elizabeth. After I'd done the course I became really assertive with my father and he couldn't understand. He could see the change in me but my mother was upset about it because she could see the change in me, too, and she didn't really like it. So she had to change as well. It caused conflict between my parents and they had to resolve it, so that's why they went to see Elizabeth.

Were you frightened of your father?

Yes, I was always frightened of my father. I remember when I was lying in bed and I could hear him in the morning or at night when he stomped down the hallway—he's very heavy-footed. That used to scare me. And I felt that I just couldn't get through to him.

So being assertive helped?

Definitely yes. I found that was one of the best things that happened. I don't know what I would have done otherwise. And I don't think I would have been able to cope at work either.

And your relationship with your parents is better?

Oh, it's much better. It's changed a lot. And now that my sister has a baby, that helps too.

In what way?

The baby gets more attention than me. My father says, 'Oh, look at this baby', and my mother loves him.

What's been the biggest change for you?

Coming out and being the person I was when I was three or four, so it's taken a long time. But there were a lot of things that had to be worked out.

What sort of work do you do now? How has your life changed?

I now teach at Murray Farm Public School as a keyboard teacher. I passed my 5th Grade piano exam. I don't know how I got through that but I think it's because I had all these positive vibes.

And you work as a consumer consultant?

Yes, I do that as well, so I have two part-time jobs. I like both of them and I wouldn't want to do anything else because I'm getting better at both jobs. My boss is happy with what I'm doing at the school and I'll be teaching more kids next year, so I'm going to be quite busy, I think. I'm doing a Diploma in Social Welfare too.

So, you're feeling fulfilled?

Yes, very fulfilled.

And are you taking your own music further?

Yes, I'm doing 6th Grade piano now and I want to be able to do that exam. I just want to see how far I can go.

Do you have other interests?

I'm doing a Psychology Course at the local community college and I find that helps in relationships with my parents and with others. I've joined a dancing group and I went by myself, so that was a bit of a challenge. I've found ballroom dancing is excellent in helping me come out of myself and to relax with men. I'm going out with somebody now who has also had schizophrenia. He's good company because he's got a sense of humour and we go out on the weekends together.

Would you say you are in love?

Oh, no. We're just friends. I think it takes time. He's probably a shy person too. But he's got a great sense of humour. It sort of overflows! He does a brickies labouring job and he's doing his HSC—he's doing English and then next year Geography, so he is doing well now, too.

Did you meet him through your work?

Yes. There was a symposium on and I actually knew him through Survey of Schizophrenia. We'd come together to have meetings about Survey Of Schizophrenia. I'd met him a couple of times before and we got along really well at the symposium. He said, 'Oh, I've been past your place'. And I said, 'Oh, you can come over some time', and I gave him my phone number.

What sort of things do you do together?

Last Saturday night we went to the movies and saw *The Bridges of Madison County*. At the end I was feeling really sad, but he said, 'Do you want a lolly?' He made me laugh. He just changed the atmosphere. And the week before we went out to dinner.

Do you plan to live away from the family home in the future?

Yes, maybe one day. I've thought about it for a long time. I got to a point where halfway through this year I was looking at places, but it would be hard to manage financially. But I've found that everything has really worked out now at home and I don't want to move away at this stage.

Tell me about your hopes for the future.

I just hope that maybe when I'm about thirty-five I'll get married and have kids . . . a couple maybe. Because, you know, I missed out on a lot. That's why I'm starting late.

What advice do you have for those who are working with people who have schizophrenia?

Be with them when they're talking about their awful state, the terrible things they've been through, it helps them through it somehow.

And what do you think is the most important aspect of recovery?

If you can accept your illness you're on your way to recovery. It took a long time for me to accept it, but once I did it gave me insights into the illness and how to deal with it. Recovery begins from that point. And just talking to a friend is important. Depending on how sick you are, it's a good idea to go away on a holiday or try socialising, but it depends on the person and whether they can handle that. Therapy with the right person is very important, too.

What is the most negative way to treat somebody with schizophrenia? What has been the worst aspect for you?

I think when people are critical of you, or they shout at you when the problem isn't your fault. I've had a lot of abuse like that. It has such a negative effect.

Criticism and abuse from what sort of people?

Parents, teachers, bosses. Criticism is the worst thing because your self-esteem just disappears.

You have insights into your illness, what else can you say about schizophrenia, ways of dealing with it, and recovery?

If someone has an episode the first thing to do is to see their doctor or therapist. It depends a lot on your choice of therapist, and how well you get on with them. It also depends very much on the individual case; some cases of schizophrenia are worse than others. With constant help, and a lot of time, I think most people can improve and many recover.

It's important to take medication. In my case I think schizophrenia was caused by a chemical imbalance. It can take weeks or months before you get to a better stage and experience the benefits. And therapy is important. Parents play a very important role, too, because you need family support.

Hospitals now are training doctors and nurses to understand schizophrenia better—there has been funding for training. At the last symposium I attended, I found that things had changed a lot in the last five years.

How would you describe yourself now?

Perhaps you never really completely recover. I don't know. But if you can accept your illness, you're on your way to recovery.

But these days, I feel as if I've been reborn. I feel as if I'm living the life I'm supposed to live and I'm doing what I was meant to do in life. Life has changed a lot for me and I'm very glad because it helps my mother too. She's a lot stronger than what she used to be. It was very hard for her too.

Karla Lorz

Karla is Rosemary Lorz's mother. Both Rosemary and her mother thought it was important for Karla to tell her story as well.

Karla, you and Rosemary talk very openly about the difficulties you had as a young mother and how that affected Rosemary. Could you tell me about the pressures you experienced at that time?

My mother-in-law was a very powerful woman. We were dependent on her because my husband and I worked in her factory—she was the manager of a weaving factory. She thought it was not only her job to run the factory and rule people there, but to rule the family as well. And, of course, Walter was her favourite son. There were conflicts when the children were born. My mother-in-law thought she knew better than I did, because I was very young when I was married. I was sixteen years old. I was hoping that I would get a lot of support from her, but she did not give me advice. She was a person who was striving for power and for money.

I felt a lot of pressure from the time I came to Australia from Austria in 1954 — 42 years ago.

There must have been difficulties adapting in a new country?

There were because I had finished school and I'd started an apprenticeship in Austria as a shop assistant/window decorator, I did that for two years and then all that was cut off. Suddenly I met Walter Lorz through correspondence and we got to the stage where he wanted to marry me. He came to Austria but I couldn't get out of the country because I was too young, so I had to get married first. Then we came to Australia.

ROSEMARY LORZ

How old were you when Rosemary was born?

I had my first daughter when I was nineteen, and Rosemary was born when I was twenty-six. With Evelyn I was still young and strong so things weren't too bad. Evelyn was also a very independent child from the beginning. I couldn't interfere with her life, I still can't.

But when Rosemary was born, it was a difficult birth because I needed a blood transfusion. I panicked in such a way that I thought I was going to die, and that stayed with me. I still have this kind of panic. And I was not very well when I came home from hospital. I needed help and I didn't have anybody so I had to do everything. Walter had to go back to work.

My sister was also working in the same factory with my mother-in-law and she said, 'I have to stay home a few days and look after Karla', and my mother-in-law said, 'No, she looks well enough. You don't have to stay . . .'

I was really run down then, and my nerves started to play up because at night I used to get panic attacks. I thought my heart was stopping and I rang the doctor in the middle of the night and said to him, 'Come quickly, I need help'. But it was just nerves.

My doctor sent me to a psychiatrist. I didn't know what a psychiatrist was at that time, I thought, 'What is he talking about?' And I said, 'What kind of doctor is he?' 'Oh, you can talk to him about your problems.' But I didn't go, so he was annoyed. I still had my panic attacks and next time I rang him he refused to come. So I went to a different doctor. I went to a German doctor and she explained to me then, in German, 'You have to see this is not a physical thing, it is emotional'.

So she sent me to a psychiatrist and he was German also. That was after Rosie had been born. And, of course, it was a turmoil because as a baby and young child she needed a lot of support, but I was out of it.

ILLNESS

My doctor told me that if I killed my child they would not put me in gaol, because he could see that I was not myself. In general I love children—look how I am with my grandson. Rosie sometimes gets a bit jealous, I know, because she can see the way I respond to the little boy—this is really my nature. But at that time I was a sick woman and, of course it rubbed off on Rosie.

I did terrible things to her. I was hitting her when she'd spill things or if she didn't do what I told her I would hit her. Later on when she went to kindergarten and I went to work, when I'd pick her up I was in a state of nervousness because she'd come home and I'd have to cook and prepare dinner. And then Rosie was always a little bit on the clumsy side, her balance was a bit out of focus, the doctor told me, and she tended to spill things or knock things over and that made me so angry, so she got blamed for it.

And that made her worse?

Yes. And she used to get so scared, as soon as I did 'this' with my hand she knew I was going to hit her again, because I'd hit her on the face. I can cry very much today and it wouldn't make any difference.

How long did that go on?

That went on until Rosemary was five years old. It was all during that important time. When she was four years old we had a wonderful neighbour who looked after Rosemary. And Rosie couldn't wait to get over there in the morning because she knew she would be treated right. She was a Hungarian lady and she had a baby the same age as Rosie . . . ten days younger. And I felt very sad in a way, because, when I went over to pick Rosie up, she didn't want to come home. She always knew when I was under psychiatric treatment and I used to go from one doctor to another.

Then the German psychiatrist died of a heart attack.

He used to threaten, 'Look, Karla, if you don't do this I will put you into hospital', and that scared me. But then, unfortunately, he was gone so I had to find another doctor and he was a bit softer. I went to him and he gave me tablets and that was not the same thing. Rosie noticed that there was something going on with me, she was two or three years old, and she noticed that I was taking too many tablets. I collapsed once at the table and she tried to give me a glass of water—she was only about four. She remembers that. So this was part of her early childhood.

When did you notice that Rosemary was unwell?

I really noticed when her 3rd Class teacher at school talked to me. Rosemary was eight years old then. I asked her, 'How's Rosemary?' and she said, 'To tell you the truth, she's not good at anything'. And I thought, 'Gee, what a thing to say' . . . not that I would question her. She might have been right. She was trying to tell me something because the teachers before were saying, 'Oh, she's OK. She's good'. But I had the funny feeling that she was not, because she was given easier schoolwork to do than the others, and that meant that she was not really coping. I thought that that might be the way it was, and I did not take much notice.

Walter said, 'She's probably a slow learner, she will grow out of it'. So we left it at that. But she made me think, 'My God . . .'. I thought it was a terrible thing to say but she was trying to tell me something and, you know, I was offended by it. I thought, 'What on earth is she talking about?'

Did you tell Rosemary what the teacher had said?

No, I never told her. I couldn't tell her. I could see that she was struggling. From day one at school she was always given easier work than the others. When the others could read their ABC she was still doing little snails.

What was she good at?

She was good at sport, singing—she was in the choir, but when it came down to Maths and those subjects, she found them difficult.

Later on as a teenager, how was she coping?

When she started high school we thought it would be turning a new leaf—she'd be at a new school with new teachers and she would probably come out of it. We thought everything would be all right. But then she became friends with a girl who was American, she was here for three years, and that girl was very strong and very clever and they became friends.

Gabrielle must have noticed something about Rosie because she was with her all the time. She was like a mother, she used to ring her up all the time after school. I got really mad. They were really very good friends. But Gabrielle was a very forward girl and she was not very popular with the teachers because she was too smart and she was also smoking marijuana. I didn't know it at the time. I found that out later. Her mother was a schoolteacher.

Rosie was the only one who was a really good friend to her. Rosie kept holding on to her because she made her feel strong. And a disaster happened when Gabrielle left, because Rosie had no friends at school, nobody wanted to be her friend. That was in Year 9 when she was fourteen.

Then we were invited to go overseas in 1979 and we left Rosie here with her sister and our son-in-law and actually at that time she improved. When we came back she was very good. She was outgoing. Her father never had time for her because he was busy. Our son-in-law understood her. He took her to Luna Park and they had fun together . . . something she'd never had. And she did extra well in school, she was well-spoken and very outgoing. But, of course, things changed, because they had their own life to live. They moved away, then Peter never had time and things went back to the old ways.

Did Rosemary talk to you about her problems or symptoms?

I had noticed that when we went out somewhere she never spoke, she was always very quiet, she never said anything. I said, 'Why doesn't she open her mouth?' Sometimes when Walter was working for the German/Austrian Society we went in the afternoon to the club, there were friends there and Rosie would only say, 'Yeah. Yeah. Yeah.' That's all she could say. I said to Walter, 'There's something not right,' And Walter said, 'She's just shy' . . . again the same story. But inside I always felt that there was something not right.

Did you think it was shyness or poor self-esteem?

I couldn't understand it. To tell you the truth, I don't know why I didn't, but I should have done something. I should have taken her to the doctor. I worried myself sick but I felt there was nothing I could do. I would talk to Walter and I talked to Evelyn and they said, 'That's probably how Rosie is'.

Until one day, we went into town to buy her some shoes, then we went to have coffee, and suddenly she said, 'There's this lady. She's here and she's talking to me.' And I said, 'What lady?' 'Yes, she loves me and she calls me "my baby"'. I said, 'Rosie, what are you talking about?' and then she told me about the voices and I thought, 'This is definitely it now. This can't be right.' And she said, 'Yes, but this is normal and she's protecting me'. She felt that it was all right that that lady was protecting her . . . she was her strength. And that's what kept her going.

What did you do then?

I took her to the doctor because I thought that couldn't be normal. I took her to the medical centre and she saw a psychiatrist. I had already been to see him and I had told him about Rosie but he did not say it was schizophrenia. They're very careful about it, they don't say it straight away. He only asked me some questions and I told him that she was hearing . . . I never knew what it was. And he gave her some tablets. And then after that things got worse. Her boss rang me from work—he was the personnel officer at Sydney Tech and Rosie was in the counselling unit—and said, 'I don't want to alarm you but I think you should take Rosie to a specialist. I think that Rosie has some sort of chemical imbalance in her brain', that's what he called it. 'The best thing is to take her to a psychiatrist, she'll probably need some medication and it will all be sorted out'.

But he didn't want to alarm me, he was very calm. That's when we went to see another psychiatrist. In the beginning she didn't tell her about the voices. That was in 1986 and she was given antidepressants.

Then we went to Europe in 1986 and she couldn't cope at all. She didn't know what to say, she didn't know whether to sit down or stand up. She made strange movements. My brother remarked, 'How different she is from Evelyn', because Evelyn was very outgoing, and he said, 'What's the matter with Rosie?' and I said, 'At the moment she's depressed and she's on medication'. Anyhow, it was a very hard time for Rosie in 1986 and she still hadn't been diagnosed with schizophrenia. It was a long time before that happened. She just got worse and worse.

Somebody at work gave her a pamphlet on schizophrenia and she had that on her desk upstairs in her room. I looked at it and I thought, 'That's a little bit like Rosie, I wonder if she's got that'. And then I rang her doctor and asked her if she thought Rosemary might have schizophrenia?' She said, 'Oh, no. Rosemary is only very depressed . . .' And I thought, 'She's a doctor, so she must know'.

So I let it go again. But we still didn't know about the

voices at that time, and then when it was found out that she was hearing voices, the doctor called me in and told me that Rosemary was very ill—she had schizophrenia.

Was her medication changed then?

We sent her to see her doctor every week. And they said that she had to leave work, so she left in 1989. And every time we saw her doctor she increased the medication. It affected her in that she was like a zombie—she couldn't walk properly. When I asked her to fold up the washing, she couldn't. She got stiff . . . she looked as if she was not all there. And when she ate she couldn't pick up her fork and knife properly. Walter saw this and he said, 'My goodness, we can't let this go on. What's happening?'

When I told her doctor, she said, 'Look, Rosemary is very ill, she needs that medication, she needs those doses. If Rosemary was admitted to a hospital she would get better more quickly, but she would be on a higher dosage of drugs. She would be sleeping all day and all night.' We thought that we'd have to accept that, but then the doctor gave her another tablet and that helped her, she loosened up a bit and she was not as stiff, she could eat and was moving better.

But when we went shopping to the supermarket sometimes she was stomping with her feet in the queue. And I'd ask her to stop it and she couldn't; it was all side-effects from the drugs. I was grateful that her doctor did not put Rosemary into the hospital because we were not privately insured. She said that in a private hospital they would look after her much better, but in a public hospital that they didn't care, they have so many patients that they can't look after everybody properly.

When did you begin to see an improvement in Rosemary?

We heard about this Young Peoples' Program at Hornsby Hospital so I rang the hospital and they said that she couldn't get in because we lived out of the area, and they said to try Cumberland Hospital.

So we tried Cumberland and they said we could go for an interview to see if she could get into the program. We saw the social worker, and we were with her for nearly two hours. There was also a psychiatrist with her and they took notes, then they said that Rosemary could go on the program. She had to go every day. I took her there in my car every morning at 9 o'clock and I picked her up at 4 o'clock in the afternoon. She was there for six months.

And what did you notice over that period of time?
She came out of herself. She was like a child . . . her mind was like a child. They tried everything to find out what she liked, so she did football and tennis, they climbed trees, washed cars and did a whole lot of things.

And you began to see an improvement?
Yes, because when she came home she started talking. And I was amazed that she was talking again.

Was her medication reduced at that stage?
The doctor at that hospital said to Rosie, 'You're taking a cocktail of tablets here, we're going to reduce them now and you will also go onto this program', and when she was on the program she didn't need to take all those tablets because suddenly there were all these people looking after her. And she had psychotherapy, psycho-education and art therapy, cooking and social skills. She really improved. Rosie had a friend, Josie, who was also a schizophrenic from an Italian family, who hated going there, she got more depressed. But not Rosemary.

Did your relationship with Rosemary also improve during that time?
Yes. I got better too. I became more and more myself again and I realised what had happened. We became very

close and I really tried to help her in every way—she became Number One. Perhaps Rosemary had a tendency to schizophrenia from the time she was a baby. But if I'd been a responsible and well-adjusted mother I would have treated her differently. So I think my treatment of her when she was a little girl made her worse.

Did you think that her recovery began when she started going to the Young Peoples' Program? Can you tell me what changes you saw in Rosemary?

Yes it did. After that time she was so motivated that she wanted to go back to work and she looked in the paper for employment. She wanted to be a secretary again. She went to a volunteer centre and she did voluntary work everywhere. They liked her because she was always available, she never missed a day. I can't remember all the things she did but it was clerical work . . . nothing complicated, a little bit of typing now and again. She always had troubles with the phones because she had a few problems expressing herself. In the program it was easy for her, but in the real world it was a different story unless people knew what was happening to her, but she didn't want to tell them because of her pride.

Did she feel ashamed of her illness?

Yes, she did, because she came home and said, 'Mum, I feel like I am ten years behind, because keeping up with today's world is not easy for me'. But that improved because she began other therapy.

Tell me about her recovery and what she's done since that time?

From there she got a job, her first typing job. That was in 1992. But then she had a relapse and she went back into therapy. At that time she was put on Prozac as well, and that helped.

And then in 1994 it was very interesting because Walter retired in 1991 and he used to say, 'Why don't we go on a trip?' Anyway we went on a trip to Malaysia in March 1994 and Rosie said that she would find a job, that she would look through the papers and that she really wanted to work, she really wanted to make money. She felt strong again after the course she'd done and so I let her go.

We went away for ten days but we kept in touch on the telephone. She never mentioned anything on the phone and when we came back after ten days she said, 'Mum I've got a job!' I asked what kind of a job and she said she had a music job.

In 1989 I had encouraged her to take up piano, so she started and continued taking lessons. She had started piano lessons when I was sick, but I didn't encourage her then, I kept telling her she was no good and that she couldn't do it.

Anyway, this time I encouraged her and I was behind her. She told me that she had a job at her old school—where she used to go as a child, and she was teaching the little kids there. She's doing very well. We are good friends with her boss, he comes here sometimes and keeps in contact on the phone.

And what about her work in the hospital?

To tell you the truth, I was a bit reluctant about that, I didn't think she would be able to do it. I didn't think she would be able to cope with talking to patients. She is a Consumer Consultant. And when she came home with an identity card, I said, 'But you're not qualified. You have to go to school, you have to have a certificate.' And she said, 'It's not like that. I am helping the mentally ill. I tell them my story. I tell them what I went through and that helps them, it encourages them.' They think, if she's done it, why can't they?

So she's a positive role model.

Yes. Of course, there are some who are very sick, but she's not involved with them. She sees people who have made some recovery. That's what she's doing now. She's come out of herself a lot. I would have to be honest and say that she is not totally recovered—she is not fully 100 per cent. It will still take time. But with time and patience and love and encouragement, I think she will get there. I must say I am very proud of her, when I look at her sometimes I think, Good on you!

12

Alan Rosen

Dr Alan Rosen is Director of the Royal North Shore Hospital and Community Adult Mental Health Services and Associate Professor and Clinical Senior Lecturer at the Universities of Sydney and Wollongong.

Rosemary Lorz, whom I've interviewed, feels that she has recovered from schizophrenia. What is your view of recovery?

Richard Warner's definitions of recovery from his excellent book *Recovery from Schizophrenia* may be a useful starting point. Complete recovery is defined as: 'Loss of symptoms of psychosis and return to the pre-illness level of functioning and ability.' And social recovery is defined as: 'Economic and residential independence and low social disruption. This means working adequately to provide for oneself and not being dependent on others for basic needs or housing. This term is the one most open to variations in measurement.'

I think the reason why we had services that were institutionally based was that we were brought up to think, through the literature, that schizophrenia was basically a lifelong disease which was, on the whole, erosive of the person, so that finally they smouldered on for years or burnt out. And there is the whole imagery around the disorder. Instead of saying that somebody 'has schizophrenia', we call them a 'schizophrenic', as if it was a label across their forehead. Professor Pilowsky from the University of Adelaide has campaigned for years about not using that term because it suggests a life sentence or, even worse, a death sentence. It objectifies that person, places the flaw inside the individual so they can't get it out.

Some of the work of people like Courtney Harding in the USA and Professor John Strauss from Yale shows that people with prolonged schizophrenia—whom we used to think had a dismal outlook—do much better than we thought. And, like some other disorders, we started realising that it worked by the rule of threes—that a third of people recovered, sometimes completely; a third of people could attain a social recovery where they could get control of the disorder and, with judicious use of medication, control the episodes and carry on reasonable lives. And a third of the people had prolonged or deteriorating courses.

But a lot of the excitement in recent years has come out of that last third where we now realise that, with a range of services available in the community, there can be much more hopeful outcomes. For example, by working towards social integration in the whole community, not just treating them with others with mental illness, by having more people in their own accommodation, integrating them into workplaces where there are people who don't have a mental illness, and into leisure facilities where there are not just other people with mental illness, they begin to feel that they have full membership of the community again.

Together with our responsiveness to crises, with their case managers from locally integrated community and hospital teams supporting them through these tasks, then, possibly, people in that last third can experience better outcomes.

Also, if you provide the range of services for people while they need them, they might outgrow you. But they need the help through the most buffeting years, and the access to help through the following years. Some people always need your help: you need to be accessible but you need to be in the background of their lives, not the foreground.

And you also need to be able to reach out to people even when they're not aware that they're unwell. You've got to ride that very delicate balance between respecting their right to privacy and at the same time saying to them, 'I won't let you do this to yourself'. Somebody has got to say, 'The buck stops here and I'll stick by you'. Extended families used to look after their own, and communities need to do that now, as they did in the past. And we've got to find systematic ways of making that happen.

Quoting a brief extract from a paper you gave to a conference in 1994, you said, 'We mental health professionals have colluded in a systematic colonising of the mentally ill, by becoming their politically anointed custodians or foster families, "for their own good".

'In the process we've inadvertently broken their spirits, disempowered them and their families, and de-skilled the community from knowing how to look after their own.

'Aboriginal and Maori people have had to contend with this on more than one front. Not only have they been dispossessed by white society, but also they have often been dispossessed of appropriate and effective mental health care. It is time that service users reclaim title to their own mental health territory.'

Now, they're pretty strong words. Can you elaborate?

The first issue was, Who owns the mentally ill? Mental health professionals have felt that we have been the spokespeople for the mentally ill, that we've been looking after them, therefore we know what's best for them and we should decide what services they need. It's more or less replacing a parental role, but it's on a lifelong basis. We did this in institutions and even when we first moved into community centred services. We've still got the legacy of our early training to contend with.

But over time we've realised—or some of us are realising—that if we put down a list of what people with mental illness need, then that list would be very different to what *they* think they need. And it would be different again from what families feel that they need.

We may concentrate on symptomatic relief and symptomatic treatments and, if not achieving cure, at least aim for maintenance and control of symptoms. And we would also be looking at relief from suffering, but they're basically fairly narrow clinical terms.

We might speculate, if not pontificate, on what their functional needs are in the community, what sort of housing they need. We might decide that they need to live in our residentials. Whereas, if you ask the consumer, most of them want to live in their own home, unbeholden to mental health professionals, and the services that we run through our hospitals and community health services.

We might think that the most important thing that they can do is get their medication right whereas for many of them their priority is paid work. Once we've developed work co-operatives and supportive employment programs where people start getting real pay, above award rates for real work, then they don't have to identify as an invalid pensioner or a disabled person but can say, 'I've had some training in house painting or landscaping, and that's what I can do'.

What was happening to families of psychiatric inpatients was that they were rarely seen by clinicians, and even then only as part of the initial assessment. They'd usually see the most junior member of the team, a social worker or a junior resident or a student. They'd get plundered for information and never be seen again. They couldn't get access to the decision makers.

But they needed support too; they needed explanation and education, they needed to know what was going on. They had expertise about what sends a service user into a spin or into a relapse, and what actually helps or protects them from going into one. Being excluded meant that families were being de-skilled, in the same way it was de-skilling the community because all the treatment occurred behind high walls, so the mentally ill became a mystery or forgotten.

Our institutions were built usually on the periphery of the communities, on the margins of the society, which dramatised the marginalisation of these people, protected the community from the mentally ill with their high walls but also de-skilled them from learning how to look after their own.

One of the most rewarding things a community can do is to feel that we look after our own, including the most disabled and the most unusual, and the whole range of people in a community. That's something we used to do before we were more complex societies, before we were de-skilled.

The other aspect of how we became less able—anthropologically or historically—was to shift from being extended families to nuclear families where everybody goes out to do something during the day and there was nobody left as support or a safety net to help people along who couldn't fully look after themselves.

And at the same time, we stopped providing valued roles in our community for people who were disabled psychiatrically. In less developed or non-industrialised societies, particularly in rural areas, there is always something you can do that's productive in a subsistence economy. You don't lose membership of that community so easily. You have an extended kinship network that can sustain you and you can share the impact of unusual or intrusive behaviours so one particular nuclear family doesn't get frazzled by it.

And in some of those communities, if your communication skills aren't too bad, and you have delusional thoughts or you're hearing voices, some people think that that's an omen for the community. If your social functioning is good and you have symptoms of schizophrenia, you might be a Shaman or an oracle in that community. So some of your experiences may be valued whereas we devalue them in Western society because we are dominated by having to be rational about what we do, or at least to be able to rationalise our passions, dreams and unusual experiences into an occupational pigeon-hole like 'I am an artist' or 'I am a mental patient'.

So it's no wonder that we can look at some of the evidence that the World Health Organisation has produced which shows that in those non-industrial societies, the rate of recovery from schizophrenia is better, or as Richard Warner concludes, at least no worse, despite the lack of modern treatment and facilities.

What is your vision for services which could be available to all those with psychiatric illness?

I think one of the things that we have to do is integrate the various needs of a person's life and not just the appropriate treatment for the illness. We must provide services to meet the person's clinical needs, functional impairment and areas of disability and handicap. If we're looking at the impairment, we'd be looking at how people might be able to process information more readily, be more attentive, be able to concentrate better. If we were talking about the disability, we might be talking about how people can relate to the world of relationships and of work and of leisure and how to use their time more effectively—how to develop some sense of mastery over their environment without being exploited. If we were talking about handicap we'd be talking about how to overcome barriers to equal membership of the community if they're stigmatised, stereotyped, discriminated against or excluded, lack access to work, to facilities, to relationships because somebody knows about their mental illness or because they appear mentally ill. So, I wouldn't restrict what services are about these days to that of 'treatment'.

What happened to people with mental illness in the past, when I was being socialised through medicine and psychiatry, was that people often became stuck in institutions. In New South Wales by 1984 we'd done a study which showed that 90 per cent of individuals with mental illness were living somewhere in the community, but 90 per cent of the resources remained in the hospitals well after de-institutionalisation had occurred. The dollars and the professional staff had to follow the patients into the community before adequate community care could be established. And over the same period, it was realised through research that people preferred to be living in the community, even if they lived in fairly grotty circumstances.

So there's something about hospital that was inherently oppressive to people no matter how much they provided this cocoon of care around them. But there was also something inherently healing about living in the community, something preferable—even if you didn't provide the services.

Then the question was: what if you provided not just short-term or narrow-focused treatment, but provided that whole system of care for people who couldn't organise for themselves? That is, a coherent system of care in the community.

There's a typology of integration, starting with integration in anthropological time which includes how to make a system in the community, how to draw those fragments together, firstly in the time slice of the present. It involves health services providing an integrated network of care equivalent anthropologically to the extended family or kinship system.

Secondly, integrating time by drawing together dislocated episodes and life disruptions through mental illness into a continuity. In the time cycle through from the past to the present to the future we should look at how to help people move through their age-appropriate transitions or rites of passage, and how to provide continuity of care—sticking by people through the critical points in their lives so that they will feel that they can approach you again or keep approaching you with confidence when they have further crises or episodes, knowing that you're not going to automatically put them in hospital, unless they particularly want or need to be there.

Integrated system building is the cornerstone of such services. There is crisis intervention in time of personal or family crisis. Then there is case management and how to provide the continuity of care through a relationship. The local psychiatric in-patient unit is an essential element of this system, but no longer the central pillar.

The other building blocks include rehabilitation services, from drop-in centres to club houses to programs to re-skill people, residential services for people who need a bridge from or an alternative to hospital admission to the community, or as an alternative to hospital admission.

Work programs—and not just play-work but real work for real pay—where you're not only helping people out financially who may not be in a good position to earn, or don't feel that they're organised enough to earn, but also restoring the dignity of their having a culturally valued role in our society.

Another building block of service is services for families and involvement of service users—involving them in running services and the management of our services so that we have a direct input into the direction of our services and to the expression of those needs into the planning of our services.

It seems to me that despite the services that are available, there are some people who still won't be helped, who will be misdiagnosed.

It took a long time for Rosemary, for example, to find any sort of appropriate service and, frankly, I think she's done quite a lot on her own and much of that has been in recent years. So, we're not suggesting at the moment that these services are available to all and that it's a perfect system.

No, not at all. And in fact, it raises two issues: The first one is how do you reach people early? How do you detect mental illness early and intervene early in a way that potential service users find appropriate, not just in a way that service providers think is appropriate. And the second issue is how do you design services for people who don't want treatment? They're sort of overlapping, but two different sets of issues.

We're working on evidence from Pat McGorry's group in Melbourne and other researchers around the world, that people do better if you intervene early. Some of the key points of those sorts of early intervention programs are things like providing services that don't diagnose people particularly as schizophrenic or manic depressive but say, 'Look, this is a young person with psychosis, we won't go beyond that because your diagnosis may change with time and there is a wide range of possible (mostly hopeful) outcomes, so we won't apply a lifelong sticky label.'

They are things like an approach in counselling that says to the person, 'Look, this is a problem in your life but it is surmountable, it doesn't have to define you. You don't have to wear it as the central feature of your identity at a time when you're forming your identity.'

And ask, how can you find meaning for this in your life so that it's not just a waste of your time and disruption of all your relationships and of your career and your studies? How can you find a meaning for this so that you can use it and then carry on with your life? And how can you then get help with appropriate medication and low-key, low-dose strategies so you don't get overwhelmed by side-effects, and you don't run a mile from treatment because the side-effects are worse than the cure? And clumsy treatment does get to that point.

How can we give you information and education partly through meeting with you and your family and/or multiple family education groups, but also with other young people? How can we help you join groups of other young people who are recovering from a similar experience, to show that you don't have to feel, 'Oh, well, I'm just going to be a psycho for the rest of my life'.

What are the challenges of the next decades for such community services?

The first challenge is just to endure and provide consistent services to individuals and their families despite regular organisational attempts to destabilise us through cost-cutting. The second challenge that underlies it is the budgetary one. The third one is to become partners with consumers and families, and we're not there yet. Consumers will point out to us that to be partners you've got to be able to negotiate from equal power.

The main challenge is to first of all get these services to endure. It's always easy to keep cutting back these services without people seeing. They'll see if a hospital closes, but they don't see what happens immediately if community teams go. It's the service-users and their families who feel the full impact in the first instance.

There's been a lack of hard, courageous decisions to make sure that budget cuts are targeted away from the community-based services, because as hospitals get smaller, we take more of the de-institutionalised as well as the un-institutionalised—those who spend most of their time out of hospital, even if they are homeless.

The third most exciting and crucial challenge, however, is to implement what we have been learning from consumers and their families: to be able to build empowering services and real recovery—that is, to seek the maximum common ground with them, to start sharing power by involving them directly in the management, running and planning of our services.

PART III
LOSS

13

Zalmai Haidary

A leading archaeologist in Kabul, Zalmai decided to flee Afghanistan with his family after the Russian invasion. In the attempt, he was captured and tortured.

A gentle, mild-mannered man, Zalmai still is optimistic about humankind despite the horrors of his experience. By contrast, I felt despair and anger while he recounted the story which has lingered in my memory.

LOSS

Zalmai, can you tell me what the circumstances were in Afghanistan prior to your escape?

I have to go back prior to the Russian invasion to describe what happened. Life was quite normal, peaceful, people were enjoying it—as in this country and many other peaceful countries. People had their freedom so they were happy with whatever they had. I'm not saying that Afghanistan is a developed country, but the people were happy.

They had a stable culture and a normal life. If you look at the number of Afghan migrants, not only in Australia but all over the world, prior to the Russian invasion, there were very few people who migrated overseas. And the reason was that people were happy in their own environment.

They had access to passports, they had freedom of travel, but they never wanted to leave the country for good. In some communities people migrate to try for a better life, but in the case of the Afghans, things were very simple. Apart from the camel drivers who migrated in the nineteenth century to Australia, if you look at the history of migration before the Russian invasion, there were only a dozen Afghans all over Australia.

And in 1979 the Russians invaded—people know about it, so I'm not going to talk about that. After the invasion things changed, so we were forced to develop the communist ideology and system. The people were not ready to accept that sort of heavy change—changes in the infrastructure, changes in social life, changes in the cultural life and relations and social activities—a huge upheaval. In a way the people were forced to adopt what was going on in Russia, in the Soviet Union, which was difficult to adopt because there were too many changes in a matter of months or years.

There was pressure from the government, from the ruling party, from the communist regime who were armed with weapons. They were in charge of military services, police services and all other services. Then there was a resistance that was growing gradually in the people towards those changes because they couldn't accept all that change. I'm talking of intellectual people, people in business, industries, all the students . . . so it was difficult.

I was working as a leading archaeologist, a member of the Academy of Science of Afghanistan, at the time of the invasion. I was Director-General for a research centre they called The International Centre for Kuhsan Studies, which was set up by UNESCO in Afghanistan when we were conducting archaeological research into the history and civilisation of Kushan. Kushan was a dynasty that included ancient Afghanistan, part of Soviet Central Asia, part of Iran and today's Pakistan and part of Northern India.

The Centre was set up in Afghanistan because the capital of that empire was Afghanistan in those days, and the great Emperor of that dynasty was Kanishka. Because I was an archaeologist and I was dealing with research and had a degree in journalism, I was employed as the Director-General for this research centre. I was a member of the professional staff of the Institute of Archaeology of Afghanistan as well.

The interference didn't stop at the academic level, and when the Russians told people that they wanted to bring changes in a direct way to research, which was not appropriate, I was in opposition. Naturally resistance was growing and I was part of that resistance. The Russian plan was to have an exhibition of Afghan artifacts travel from the Afghanistan National Museum and Art Gallery to the Soviet Union. And so a delegation was appointed by the Deputy Prime Minister who was also the Minister of Information and Culture.

I was in charge of that delegation to look at the possibility of sending these artifacts to the Soviet Union. When I looked at the policy in the project I found that there were some problems. First of all, there were no guarantees on an international level of insurance of the artifacts, and we wanted a few of our exhibitors to be with the exhibition in the Soviet Union. But the Russians wanted it according to their own wishes, they wanted to impose on us a program which was against our laws and regulations, even against the law for international museums.

So I approached the Minister and explained that as a responsible person in charge of this delegation, I could not take the responsibility. What if something happened to these irreplaceable items? Some of them were unique in the world.

He was not happy about it, but later on he said it was OK and that it didn't matter. But they appointed another delegation and two weeks later I was imprisoned because I was not obeying the regulation of the party, which was not true. But it was a warning to me.

For my wife's part, she was a high school teacher. She was transferred to a primary school because she was opposing the Soviet's teaching material. They even changed our national anthem. They tried to interfere in our history. She was teaching history and culture. They said that some paragraphs in the books should be blackened and she opposed it. 'This is history, we have to teach the people this. It's a reality we can't change it by cutting out the pages of the book. We cannot ignore history.'

As a result of this resistance, she was transferred to another school far from home and then was given shift work—a few hours in the morning and in the afternoon; a few hours in one school and in another school—which was against the laws of the education system in Afghanistan.

We had a little daughter, our eldest child then, she was in Year 3 of primary school. Because she was bright and intelligent, she was chosen to be sent to Russia, and we opposed that. We told them we didn't want her to go.

Who decided that she should go?

The communist school authority. We knew it was a method of brainwashing children. And we opposed it, it was not good.

Did you have any choice about whether your daughter could go?

No, no, we had no choice. And our whole family—my brother, sisters—all opposed this plan. My brother was teaching chemistry at the faculty of sciences. Another one was teaching at the college.

So all these things affected the whole family. And then a couple of my brothers escaped—they couldn't tolerate the situation. One of them went to Iran and the other went to Pakistan and from there he escaped to Germany. So I realised that there was a limited time for us and I thought that I might be arrested.

How long did you spend in gaol that first time?

It was just for three days. And it was not gaol, it was a detention centre where people were interrogated. To me this was a warning.

After that I decided to escape. It was very difficult because in the neighbourhood where we were living there were a few members of the Intelligence Services and a colleague of mine who was working in the same office with me was a party member, so it was very difficult to manage.

I realised that we were under their surveillance, especially after the escape of my brothers. We were looking for an opportunity to escape, but they had police patrolling the borders, starting from Kabul.

The pressure continued—harassment at work. We had a group of people called the political committee in each organisation. A group was appointed, a staff member and people from outside, who would come and have a political meeting, then they issued orders about what we should do and what not to do. Unfortunately, the selection of these committees was not on the basis of scientific merit, it was purely political merit.

Archaeological research was stopped in Afghanistan. There were different foreign teams we had contracted from France called D.A.F.A. (Delegation Archaeological of France and Afghanistan), which we had had for almost thirty-five years, and that was stopped. We couldn't renew those contracts.

We had British scholars who used to come to do research, Italian archaeologists, at the same time we had a Russian delegation and we had an Indian archaeologist who used to come in to do restoration work in a Buddhist monastery.

So gradually all these contacts were cut off. In the meantime there were limited resources and funding for restoration, the country was spending much of its budget on defence and secret police.

So, gradually the projects were stopped, unfinished. No matter how we tried to explain to them about the necessity of applying chemicals to the statuettes, monasteries and other places, it made no difference. In restoration work, if you do not continue maintenance, the objects will be damaged. And all these artifacts and monasteries and archaeological discoveries are for the nation. Not only the nation, they belong to the whole of humanity. But we were under the control and policing of this communist party and its members, so everything was very limited.

They considered me a traitor—you were either a member of the party or you were a traitor. You had to join the communist union, or you had to learn the Russian language. At first I resisted but finally the option I took was to study Russian, and that was after hours when I finished work. This was the mentality. We were forced to accept communism and the mentality of communism. They brought in people from rural areas, people without knowledge, and the person who was in charge of our institute was a former primary school teacher who didn't know what archaeology itself meant, or what research meant. But he was a very experienced party member and had been a member for ten to fifteen years.

So your brothers had escaped and you were planning to escape as well?

My brothers, two of our sisters, my wife, children and I, and my brother's wife and child started a joint journey to escape. At one stage my mother couldn't tolerate seeing all these things happening so she had a nervous breakdown and then finally passed away after a heart attack. It was the pressure, the stresses that she had with the whole family collapsing and her children escaping. All the time there were people coming to search our house, there were day-to-day arrests, curfew, all these sorts of things.

We planned to escape at a time of the pilgrimage to Mecca, where the people go to Mecca during a three-day public holiday. We thought that if we moved on those days there would be fewer people patrolling the border, and on the way to Jalalabad. We decided one morning to go around four o'clock, after the curfew, and travel in the back of a truck.

We arranged with this truck driver to come and get us and he said he was going to hide us amongst the load, which was wool or cotton they used to bring to Jalalabad. And he wanted a certain amount of money. We just simply left our home without touching anything—not even locking the doors.

I remember the night before, we went to see our father. All of the family gathered at my father's place, my brothers and sisters—all of us, and none of us was able to say good-bye to our father because of his emotions. We felt that he was going to disclose to a neighbour or to some person and there was no trust, the trust had gone from everybody. There was suspicion, systematic arrests . . . all these things were going on. So, that night we stayed with our father and at about 7 pm returned to our own places. The truck was supposed to come to my house, we'd get back together at 9 pm, and stay there until the morning. I remember that my youngest son and my nephew were crying, and the guy said that when we reached the border patrol he was going to knock on the back of the truck and we'd have to put tape on their mouths so they would not shout or cry.

My son was two-and-a-half and my nephew one-and-a-half years old. So we couldn't control their crying. But my daughter and my older son were eight and ten. And I remember that at one stage in the journey they were piercing the loads with these steel rods to see if there was someone or something in them, but we were fortunate because there were boxes inside the loads that we were in. It was normally a two-hour journey, but it took us almost seven hours—even longer than that to reach the city of Jalalabad which was on the Pakistan border.

There we negotiated with a group of Mujaheddin to see if they would allow us to stay in a fortification outside the city and under the control of the freedom fighters and Mujaheddin—out of the control of the government. We stayed there for three nights because it was the public holidays. Of course we all grew beards and changed our clothes and appearance. My wife wore the normal Kochi (traditional garment) and the children as well. Sometimes we'd put dirt on the faces of the children to make them look like rural people and not from the city, We didn't wash for two or three days.

Because of my continuous relationship with the Department of Information and Culture in this region—this was an excavation site on a regular basis—people knew me in the area. I knew that if I went out and I came across some people, they would tell the Intelligence and we would be arrested. And my two younger brothers were too young to go out. If they caught them in the street they would arrest them and send them into military service, which was something normal in the country. If they saw a youngster in the street, they would arrest him, put him in the back of a truck and send him direct to the battle front without telling his family.

So, I asked our eldest brother to find someone who could assist the women and children to go to the border and we men could walk. He said, OK, that he would find someone who could smuggle the women and children and he went out on the third day to find someone.

I was sitting at home with my two brothers, my wife and children, my two sisters and my brother's wife, when suddenly I saw that the fortification was surrounded by military police and secret police agents. People were climbing the walls with guns and machine guns and shouting through loudspeakers, 'DON'T MOVE. YOU HAVE BEEN SURROUNDED.'

I was shocked. And my children were terrified, wanting to know if they were going to kill us. The door was locked with a chain and they burst in and handcuffed us. They started asking us questions like, 'Who are you? Where are you from? Why did you come here? What do you want to do?'

We had some small bags with photograph albums, and I had a collection of coins and some of our qualifications—these were our valuables. We said that we'd come for a holiday. They said, 'No, you didn't come for a holiday you came here to stay, because of these photograph albums'.

My wife was quick to think and she hid my qualifications under the carpet so they didn't see them, they couldn't identify me. But my other identification papers were in my pocket, like my driver's licence, and membership card of the Academy.

They arrested us and said that we were traitors to the regime and gave us a communist-type lecture. They took all the women and put them in one room so I started shouting, 'Don't touch the children and my wife, do whatever you like with me'. And they started bashing me and kicking me on my head, on my legs, with their military boots and it was a horrible time. They kept on bashing us, punching us on the back and kicking with their boots. And then they blindfolded me and my two younger brothers, put us in the back of a jeep and took us to their interrogation centre which they called Khad centre—Khad was the name of the Intelligence Service of Afghanistan. There were three Intelligence Services, and this was a Khad centre for the police. They also had a civilian and a military one. We were caught by the Police Intelligence Service which was the worst one.

We had no idea where we were going. My kids started shouting, and they pointed their guns at them, threatening that they were going to come back and kill them. They took us to a room and we were still blindfolded. Then they took the blindfold off, we looked at each other and my younger brother asked me what we should say. I said we should say we had come for a visit, not that we came here to escape.

Then another guard came, a very strong village person. He took my brothers to another room and I was left there alone. The room had a small door with steel bars, a small window with steel bars, and it had shutters which could only be opened from the outside. Nobody gave us any food on that day. No water. Nothing. Fortunately I had a packet of cigarettes and I was smoking and moving around the room.

During the night they took us and then the interrogation started. That was a tough time. At the beginning it was a Russian interrogator. He was very gentle at first, 'Why are you doing this? You're a bright person, why are you not helping the communist regime . . . the people's regime? There will be equal opportunities for our people . . .' He gave me a lecture for about twenty minutes.

I said, 'Whatever you are telling me, I know, but I am

not what you want to prove'. He gradually became abusive, banging his fist on the desk, shouting at me and insulting me. He called my mother names and when he said this I couldn't tolerate it because my mother had passed away and I was still grieving her death. He kept insulting my mother and he threw a glass of water in my face. Then he burnt me on my back with a lighted cigarette and threw more water in my face.

I abused him with words, because I couldn't handle him insulting my mother. I should not have done it, but I was too emotional. He kept insulting her and calling me *yupto yomat*, which is not a good word . . . it means 'mother-fucker'. So that really got to me and I couldn't control myself. I repeated the same word to him, he got very abusive, and then he gave me electric shocks.

He called an Afghan guard, a big built, very strong man from the northern part of Afghanistan, and said to him, 'You're the one who is going to make him a human being'—he was speaking a mixture of Russian to him as well as Pashto. The guard was from the northern part of Afghanistan but he was able to understand it. He was a soldier who had finished his compulsory military service and was staying in the military as a regular soldier. And he was a communist, one of those who had accepted communism. He took me into another room and tied me really tightly onto a chair. He gave me electric shocks. They put wires on my toes and on the back of my neck. Then they put a very strong light in my eyes . . . it was a really terrible light. He was standing behind the light and kept asking me who I was spying for, and calling me a traitor.

In the initial stages I was resisting, and gradually I felt, 'What's the use? This person will abuse me, and the more I resist the more he will bash me up.' Then he smoked a cigarette and put it out on the back of my feet . . . it was awful to smell my skin burning . . . sometimes when I smell a barbecue it reminds me of that smell of my skin burning.

Well, that continued. I was there for twenty-one days. Every night it was the same. And for about eight or nine days they put me in acid ... they put my hands and my legs in a liquid. I don't know if it was acid, but it made me itch, and they would tie me up so that I couldn't scratch ... I don't know how to explain it but it was a very severe type of itch. It wouldn't stop. I wanted to scratch my hands and then they could kill me! But I was not allowed to scratch.

They would also bash my brothers in the room next door, and I could hear their cries ... especially the youngest one, he was very young. During the day they used to take my two brothers to be labourers. New buildings were being constructed and trucks brought bricks and mortar and they were used like slaves to do hard labour from five in the morning until seven in the evening.

They had to carry bricks, mortar, all the building materials by hand as there was no machinery to help them. During the night they were tortured, but they weren't as severely tortured as I was. They were not burnt with cigarettes, they were bashed up. And they cried out.

A week later, one night they brought them in front of me so I could see them being lashed on the back. They threw them to the ground and they lashed them on the back like animals. My younger brother kept crying and crying. It was terrible, very terrible. The older one was resisting.

My brother who had not been captured was doing everything possible so that they would release us. He tried to find some party member who was close to this person who was in charge of the interrogation service, but he couldn't. Eventually he found a freedom fighter who was a double agent and also a guard in this interrogation centre. Before that they got our files and wanted to send us to the military intelligence service by helicopter to Kabul. We were again blindfolded on that day. We used to hear that they took people in helicopters over the mountains and threw them out alive on to the mountains. It happened to many people. That was a fear that stayed with us when they blindfolded us. But the helicopters were not ready or there was something wrong with them.

The double agent finally came to us and said that he had talked to my brother who hadn't been captured, but I couldn't trust him. He said, 'You're on limited time. The next time they take you in the helicopter, you will be thrown out on the mountains, or even if they take you to Kabul, you will have the maximum twenty to twenty-five years in gaol, or they will torture you there, kill you . . . whatever is going to happen will be worse than what you are getting now. So trust me.' I replied, 'I'm sorry. I can't trust you.' But my younger brother said he would trust him. I said, 'Tell my brother, the one who sent you, to give me some specific detail or something that happened in our family . . .' I needed proof, something from the family or a specific word, something only our family would know. And then I would trust him. This was my brother who had gone out to find a safe journey for the women, so he was out the day we were captured. His name is Akbar. Now he is in Canada.

The next day the double agent came back and told me some special words from my brother. When my mother died, my brother and I had had a conversation, so he told me what we had said between us. And then I believed I could trust him. He said that there was a toilet block facing the river . . . this interrogation centre was built on the banks of the Kabul River, for security. On one side was the prison with high walls and some electric wires for security; on the back side was the river. In the far corner of this place they built the toilets for the prisoners, there were steel bars on the toilets.

The guy said that he would loosen two steel bars, in

toilet number 3. 'When you go to the toilet just stay and when you hear a knock, remember that these are your brothers, don't lock the toilet door. When your brothers join you, then take the loosened steel bars off and escape. You have got ten minutes. It'll be all right with the searchlight. Then you have to cross the river, and on the other side of the river is a free area called Barabad, because of the Mujaheddin, so nobody can touch you. And there's a guard—but we have already told him about it—he will send you his son to meet you and take you to the village and there you will be free. Then your brother will come with a group and talk to you.' I said that would be all right.

It was after midnight, 2 am, when we had arranged all this. I always remember the time, it was very late at night. I asked the guard if I could go to the toilet, he said OK, opened the door and I went to the toilet. And I waited there for a while. My other two brothers came, knocked, I let them in and at that stage I took the loosened bars off.

I jumped first. It was about four or five metres down the bank of the river and my brother dislocated his ankle, poor child. Gradually and slowly we moved down to the river and my other brother didn't know how to swim. The rocks on the banks of the river were very slippery and the water was rising up and up so we had to swim in the middle of the river to get to the other side. My young brother slipped on a rock and my other brother and I grabbed him, he was very scared. And he held on to us around our necks.

And you had very little time to make this escape?

We had very little time and we were bloodied, wounds and scratches on our bodies, feet and hands. We were like wet rats. I was not thinking about anything except survival, to get away from this torture. I was not thinking about the pain I felt in my body, not food, thirst, nothing

... the question was just to survive and get out of there. Finally we made it across to the place called Barabad.

Barabad was under the control of the Mujaheddin and there was a fellow called Gulalam who sent his son to meet us and take us to the village. They gave us a hot meal and made hot tea for us. His wife brought us some clothes and dressed my feet and gave us Vaseline for our wounds. They assured us that we would be safe there. Even if we could hear the people shouting on the other side of the wall and even if they put the lights on the river . . . we were safe.

My two brothers were still shaking with fear but they assured us that nothing else would happen to us, that this was a free area of the Mujaheddin, and that no one would come across the river to get us.

We had no news of what was going on with our families—wife and children—but I knew that my brother had survived and this guy told me that everything was OK. It was about five or six in the morning when my brother arrived. He brought us some food in a bag and said, 'I know that you are miserable and that you may not be able to move, but you have to move because this area, although it's under the control of the Mujaheddin, could be raided at any time. There is a group coming from Surkhroud—another part of Jalalabad—who are going to Pakistan. You'd better join this group. Don't worry about the women and children, I will manage that. Just escape.'

So in the morning they gave us some warm clothes and sneakers and some military boots for my brothers. It was very difficult for me to walk because of abscesses and sores on my legs. But we had to leave.

The following night we started our journey, and this was an eleven-day journey by foot with the Mujaheddin, going up and down the mountains. We came to a place called Kuttee Uttarian

My brother had arranged with another group of the Mujaheddin to take the women and children there, and

LOSS

we would join them. The Mujaheddin were not going straight there, they were zig-zagging because of the mines and the military posts. They walked through the bush and through the mountains. So we planned to join our family in a place called Manghaval in Kunner province and then we were to start the other part of our journey which was another three or four days.

On the next part of that journey we came across dead bodies with vultures feeding on them, we came across unexploded rockets in the sand and at one stage, close to the Pakistan border, a gunship helicopter chased us and we had to hide under bushes. I had wounds bleeding on my legs and especially on my back, and I had to carry my youngest son. We were starving, we had no food, just a small flask of water. It was a very terrible and miserable situation.

The last mountain was a very high mountain, and we did it, with lots of difficulty. It was a breathtaking thing to escape and travel the way we did . . . but we made it to Pakistan.

I remember that the happiest day of my life was seeing the Pakistani cars and buses with their number plates, on the other side of the mountains. There was a local tea house and when we went in they said, 'This is Pakistan'. So I thanked God. We had a rest and food for three or four days. Finally, the whole family got together in the back of this truck and travelled to Peshawar.

We thought that if we approached the Mujaheddin there we would be heroes and survivors and they would look after us. But when we talked to the officers, there were no appointments, no chance to go and see these leaders and explain what we had gone through. There was no admiration or appreciation of what we'd gone through. The attitude was, 'Thousands of people make it and thousands don't, and people have had a more serious history than you. You have to thank God that you're here, it's not our responsibility.' Then I realised that we'd been left in the middle of nowhere just with expectations.

Anyhow, we stayed there for a week and I had basic treatment at the hospital on my legs. We went to the capital city, Islamabad, and lived in a two-bedroom unit: 11 people in a small unit. There we started our lives from scratch. We had to go and buy some mats to put on the floor and some small cushions, and then we had no money. We started looking for work to survive, because you're not allowed in the refugee camp without any financial support. We had thought that if we were refugees we'd receive support from these groups. But nothing.

A week after I arrived in Islamabad I found a job at the Afghan educational centre for refugees as an English teacher, and then later on I applied for another job as a language broadcaster at Radio Pakistan. Then I found some tutorial work, teaching English at people's places. That went on for about six months.

It was good. I was working from eight in the morning until twelve midnight because my radio broadcasting was during the night. I did it to earn the money to keep my family because we were a family of eleven.

Then the whole family applied to migrate to Australia, United States and Canada. My single brothers and sisters were accepted into the US because they were single. At that stage there were privileges for people who were not married—they could go earlier, so they went to the US and I was accepted into Australia and my brother went to Canada. So we were all separated.

But it was fortunate that we spent fourteen months together in Pakistan, some people spend years there without getting a visa. And most of my healing process was in Pakistan because I was a language broadcaster and I was writing a documentary every night after the news. I was expressing what I was going through, opening up the regime for the refugees, and for people inside Afghanistan. Now I realise, of course, that broadcasting and writing were a healing process for me and I was fortunate that I could write about my experiences.

What happened when you arrived in Australia as refugees?

We arrived here in Australia on the 21st of December 1985, over ten years ago. I understood that my brother-in-law would come and meet us at the airport but he missed the telex. We were there at the airport, looking at other people with their families who came to meet them with bunches of flowers . . . and there was nobody there for us. We were there for hours and hours and I didn't even have money to make a telephone call. I had some American dollars with me but the bank was closed, so I borrowed 20 cents from a gentleman and made a phone call from the airport.

My brother-in-law apologised, he came and picked us up and took us to his place. He was living in a one-bedroom unit, which was very difficult for us: there was five of us, and we were a burden.

Then I went out and found a place to rent—a two-bedroom unit. It had no carpet, it was on the ground floor and nobody wanted to rent it because it was damp and the rooms were very small. The agent said that it needed to be painted first and I said I would do the painting. 'Please just give me the keys, because we need a place to live'.

Then I approached the Salvation Army, the Smith Family, and they said, 'You came to the right place at the wrong time. It's not a good time, people are on holidays, it's Christmas and nobody is around.' I remember that we borrowed a saucepan from a neighbour and we used to boil water for tea, fry eggs in it, cook all our food in it. We were sleeping on this wooden floor for seven days, until Christmas was over, and then it was New Year and people were still on holidays. We had two towels and gave one to the younger child to sleep on. He was two-and-a-half years old and the poor child was sick.

I had promised him that our lives would change once we got to Sydney. In Australia things would be better. One morning he said, 'Dad, Dad—in our own language—let's go, let's go'. I asked him where. He said, 'Let's go to Australia, I'm sick of this place'. I said, 'My son, this is Australia'. He said, 'You said that in Australia things were going to change, we were going to have our own bedrooms, we were going to have our own beds'. And tears poured from my eyes. I thought, 'This poor child, he is still experiencing all those horrible times . . .' Well, it was a struggle for survival, establishing a new life from scratch, having a new identity in a country with lots of differences. It was a culture shock. For me it was OK because I'd travelled through Europe and in many other countries, but for my wife and kids it was a new experience, in terms of language, culture, new environment, lack of support, lack of having an identity in a foreign country, and not knowing anyone.

It was a very stressful situation, at least for our first four or five months. And then when I sent my qualifications for assessment—I have a Bachelor and a Masters degree—the first blow was that they were considered equivalent to two years of tertiary education in Australia. It had taken ten years, but they were the equivalent of two years. I had published at least twenty or thirty articles at an international level. I'd published a book, *The Coins of Kushan*. So I had to start from scratch. I tried every single place. I knocked on every single door. I knew that there was a place called CES and that it was a responsible organisation that provided jobs. So I kept pestering them, going every day, but they couldn't get a job for me. The only thing they could do was write me a résumé. I went to different places for different jobs—to museums and other places—but I had not one single response. I had no references, no referees, I didn't know anybody, I had no local experience. For some jobs I was over-qualified, for others under-qualified. There was a direct market company and I started working with them distributing leaflets and pamphlets and paper for them, and they paid me fifteen to twenty dollars per week for distributing their leaflets. My wife helped me too.

I could speak six languages so I thought perhaps I could use these skills. The CES suggested I approach the Ethnic Affairs Commission or Immigration, and finally I was employed as a casual translator for the Ethnic Affairs Commission and the Department of Immigration Telephone Interpreter Service.

But I hardly got jobs because I was new and I had no references. Gradually, though, I started getting translating jobs; people would bring their documents for translation—marriage certificates and things like that. It was a low-paid job. I was getting about $8.50 for each job. I had to deliver the job myself and take the job myself from the office, so I had to travel and spend $2 to get a job because the Ethnic Affairs Commission was in the City. So I had to pay fares. And sometimes they criticised me because I was not typing the translations, I wrote them by hand because I had no typewriter. They said that they would pay me a $1 less because they had to type it themselves, so they paid $7.50 for hand-written ones.

But that's the way that I started interpreting and translating. And then I was trying to do something for the Afghans, we were in the process of establishing a community, the people were migrating under compassionate grounds as refugees.

One day I was visiting an Afghan family who were living close by and had been there for two years and I wanted to go and learn from their experiences. They showed me this letter from Careforce which mentioned that The Australian Council of Churches had given some funds for Afghans to establish a community organisation.

They wanted to know if anyone was interested in getting together to talk about their experiences because they wanted to learn about the new arrivals' experiences to see what sort of services they might need. I went to that meeting and the next day I came home and talked to the social worker at Careforce about the difficulties and she was very interested because I had genuine difficulties.

From that time I became involved with this voluntary group. We developed a constitution for the Afghan community and the establishment of a community organisation. It was a lot of hard work in establishing that. In the meantime I was doing this junk mail distribution and translating now and then.

I had post-trauma stress symptoms, I got flashbacks, irritation. And I had feelings of worthlessness, because I used to be something in my country and I was nothing here. People hardly knew me. So how could I prove myself?

It must have all seemed so futile in those early days.

That's right. But I never lost hope. The time I was in gaol there was a hope in me that things might change. And that hope made me strong. That was part of my strength.

How important do you think hope was in your survival?

I think I had an inner strength. My younger brother had more strength than the older one. The younger one was imitating me but the older one was analysing himself. I had to encourage his survival, whereas the younger one trusted in what I believed. He had great strength, he was not scared for his own survival, he was looking out to make sure that his older brother survived too. I believed that I was not going to die, that I had to survive because my family was there and my younger child needed me. I was not going to die, and I didn't accept that I would die.

Did you always have a sense that things were going to get better?

Yes. There is always a light at the end of the tunnel, but you have to accept the darkness when you travel to the end of that tunnel, and have the guts to accept the pressures. I remember a couple of nights before coming to Australia I was in an elated mood. I was thinking that I was leaving everything behind—the torture, the trauma, the experiences, the migration, the bad stuff, mass-killing ... everything, whatever was going on there. I was totally empty, there was nothing on my chest.

But when I came here suddenly all these things mounted up on each other. When I came here my son was playing at school and I got a telephone call from the teacher to say he had a fractured arm and, you wouldn't believe it, I was carrying my son on my shoulders, and he was almost nine years old. I was carrying him because there were no taxis to the Western Suburbs Hospital. He was crying on my shoulder, 'Dad, let me walk. You are tired, and you're hardly breathing, you're sweating, let me down.' I said, 'No, I'm going to carry you because if I let you down you will damage yourself'. I was full of pain and stress. My past experiences flooded back.

Tell me about your work with the Service for the Treatment and Rehabilitation of Torture and Trauma Survivors (STARTTS). How did that begin?

I was working as a social worker for the Afghan community. In our culture, people who have got qualifications and experience have a name in Afghanistan; there's a sign of respect so people pushed me to take that position. When I was working for this community organisation I was asked to do a session on torture and trauma issues. We talked about the torture and trauma experiences the Afghan suffered, and their migration. And then I was asked if I could start working on a part-time basis with STARTTS.

It was in February 1989 that I officially joined them. Gradually the number of clients increased, so I began working two days a week.

And gradually I developed some skills in psychotherapy

counselling—they used to call it 'bicultural counselling' in those days. In 1991 I was working for two communities, the Afghans and the Iranians, because I could speak Persian. I'd been in Iran a few times so it was easy for me to learn. And gradually the position changed from that to Middle Eastern bicultural counsellor, which included Kurdish, Assyrian and Iraqi, because there were different people coming from Iran, Baha'is, Kurds . . . there was a great need for a Middle Eastern worker. I am now Counsellor/Team Leader.

Your work now is totally different to what your work was in Afghanistan.

I joke with friends sometimes and say, 'The digging is the same. Over there I used to dig the ground, now I'm digging the people.'

Through your experiences you are obviously able to help other people. Would you say that you've put your own experiences of torture, having to leave your country and culture, in the past?

Yes. There are two things—one is a memory, and as part of my memory I can't forget it. If I could forget it I would not have been able to talk to you about it today. But how to analyse these memories and understand what has happened to you, that's the important thing. Some people in our culture, in Middle Eastern culture generally think that if you don't talk about it you might forget it. They say, 'Let's not talk about it, because it's not good, it's bad. It might make us miserable.' Which is not true. If you don't talk about it, it's always there, in the back of your mind and it will come back now and then in nightmares, in flashbacks, and in different ways. But if you talk about it and analyse it and realise what happened and keep it as a memory of your past, then it will not visit you in your day-to-day life. This is the important thing.

But, you know this concept of counselling and psychotherapy is a new concept, not only for Afghans, but for all people from the Middle East, because there were other means that existed in the community.

What were they?

Talking to a neighbour, talking to a friend, talking to a family member, a brother, sister, someone who is close by. And for elderly people, going to the corner shop and sitting there, buying a newspaper or bottle of milk and talking with the shopkeeper, dealing with groups, friends. Ritual links . . . visiting shrines, graves, mausoleums . . . the ritual that goes with that. Rituals like praying, and believing in God bring them some calmness inside.

A network of family support is very important, but it is not here. In all those countries, the psychological services are very few. You have very few psychologists, because they have no clients. People are not approaching them because they have other means. So my approach with a client is psycho-education. After establishing a rapport with a client I will tell them, 'Look, in this country you have very limited family support or no family support. If you want to survive, these are the means and the ways.'

How would you describe your life now?

Now I've got over all those experiences. I admitted to myself that they happened, they are part of my past like my education, my marriage, my social life back home, my family, the environment that I had. Everyone has got good and bad experiences in their lives.

I feel happy as a normal person. I consider myself a citizen of this country. I think I've got freedom—freedom of speech, freedom of choice. I've got a job. I've got my family. My children are continuing their education. Sometimes I might think that I have changed my career, but it happens. I was an archaeologist, now I am not. But I am doing something that's worthwhile, I'm helping people. And when I go home I have a feeling of satisfaction that

I have done something for people, something that they need, it makes me happier.

On top of that I have a job, wages, I've established myself. I've got a house that I live in with my wife and my children. Everybody's needs have been fulfilled and that is living well. I have made contact with my other family members, bearing in mind that even back home if we were all together we would be living separately. Now if I want to contact them I can, they can come here or I can go there. Yes, my life is good.

14

Margaret Cunningham

Margaret Cunningham is Executive Director of STARTTS—Service for the Treatment and Rehabilitation of Torture and Trauma Survivors.

How is torture defined?

Torture practices usually happen through a multiplicity of experiences, so although I'm listing them, often people have had up to seven of these experiences at one time.

People may have been exposed to burning, humiliation, sexual violation, beatings, starvation, bondage, electrical torture. They may have also witnessed other people being tortured, witnessing the rape of children, witnessing people's limbs and parts of their bodies being chopped off or being placed in a situation where they're hearing screams—mock executions—where people are prepared for their own death and it's suddenly called off. There is a whole range.

We know that the systematic use of rape in the former Yugoslavia is beyond what people have reported in previous holocausts. They also experience loss of family members, the murder of family members, violations at all levels. The aim of torture isn't about just getting information, it's about trying to destroy a person's capacity to function as a member of society.

Why was STARTTS formed in Australia?

Some concern had been raised by ethnic health workers in the Department of Health in Western Sydney that, despite access and equity and equal employment opportunity-types of programs, people in some of the ethnic communities (regardless of whether the policies of access and equity were achieved by a Community Health Centre or a hospital) still felt uncomfortable accessing a service because of some of the experiences they'd had in their own country. So in New South Wales, a research program was undertaken on the health-care needs of victims of torture, looking at it from a health perspective.

What came out of that study?

What came out of it was indeed what ethnic health workers had said—that people were carrying levels of trauma with physical problems as well as emotional problems as the result of torture experiences, and that workers in the health system weren't identifying it.

That document actually received acclaim world-wide. The research was designed to establish some service provision. Prior to this research, concerns had been raised for a number of years that there was no specialised care for refugees who were torture survivors.

What sort of numbers are we talking about at that time?

In 1988 we knew that Australia had taken about half a million refugees from the end of World War II. At that time it was also reported that somewhere around 20 per cent of refugees were likely to have a torture experience.

Can you tell me about the work of STARTTS?

In 1988 the main areas for the work were: to begin developing the knowledge within Australia of working with refugee families who were torture survivors; to develop treatment programs which enabled families to access them; to develop research programs and be part of the international network of torture and trauma survivors. That was the mandate in those very early days. I became the director of the service after about six to nine months. One of the concerns I had was that I think there are many people who do have emotional and psychological problems as a result of the experiences they've had, but it doesn't mean that they're not functioning in some other areas of their life, and it doesn't mean that they can't go on to function.

We also began to look at the appropriateness of only developing individual Western-styled approaches to working with clients in what is essentially the talking cure—which is another terminology for psychoanalysis or psychotherapy. When you're working with communities which don't have sophistication and language, that isn't always possible or appropriate.

Some communities don't even have a word for going to someone to whom you're not related and telling them your personal problems. So there needed to be a whole different way of accessing some of those communities. Right from the beginning at STARTTS, we built our services around bicultural counsellors. We felt that it was important to have people on staff who reflected the communities we were working with, and not just interpreting or in a minor role to Anglo practitioners, but that their voice about treatment approaches and ways of working with the communities needed to be honoured and validated in the program.

I was also interested in group work and how people can heal in group processes. I was very concerned about some of the literature which said that you can't run groups with refugees and torture survivors—they're too damaged to be able to utilise that as a process. I was very critical of that view. We do run programs that are multicultural. And we see it as important to include community development and advocacy approaches.

I imagine that some care is needed in the selection process for these groups?

Well, yes. But our children's camps, for example, have Bosnian and Serbian children involved together in the programs. I think that part of our responsibility is not to get into the debate about who has been most or least tortured. Torture is a world-wide entity; torture happens everywhere.

What sort of people make up the team at STARTTS?

We have psychiatrists, psychologists, social workers and a physiotherapist. We're also open to traditional forms of medicine such as acupuncture and Chinese medicine. And the team is from very diverse backgrounds. When we began STARTTS there were no qualified psychologists, social workers or medical practitioners in the Cambodian community, they'd all been killed off and those resources weren't here. So we had to identify people who we felt could be trained to work in a clinical way, and so some of our bicultural staff have qualified in those areas. Some of them have gone on to do degrees here, in welfare or welfare associated studies, and we've developed our own training programs to skill people up in assessment referral and counselling processes. So currently we have staff in the agency who reflect the Vietnamese, Laos-Cambodian, Latin-American, East-Timorese and Afghan-Iranian communities, Middle Eastern communities and former Yugoslavs.

In terms of the work we do, we have programs providing people with counselling and we assist people to access other health facilities or other services that are more appropriate. We also have children's programs and facilitate camp programs which we conduct two or three times a year. We've now got a full-time youth worker so we've been able to put much more emphasis into that program.

Have the problems of refugee children been overlooked in the past?

Yes. Refugee children have been overlooked world-wide. And there are some workers at STARTTS who have clinical skills in working with children, and they do see children, but at the time we developed this camp program, we didn't have the resources to set up a children's clinic, so we felt that this was at least one way of beginning to access kids we were concerned about.

When the service was first set up where were torture and trauma survivors predominantly from?

Mostly Spanish-speaking, people from El Salvador and Chile. Also Vietnam, Cambodia and Laos.

And since then?

We've continued to see those communities because the nature of working in this field is that people may actually experience difficulties even up to twenty years after the experience. At the moment we are seeing lots of people from the former Yugoslavia, people from African states are accessing the service, those from East Timor who are living in Sydney, people from all of the communities of the former Yugoslavia, so it's not just the Bosnians. We're also working with people from the Serbian and Croatian communities.

How difficult is it for people who have experienced torture to actually talk about it or come forward?

It can be very difficult. For people in some communities there is a fear of being seen as crazy. They don't want to approach a service because of the stigma that may be associated with it in their own countries.

We also try to look at the skills people use to survive, if they're still using those skills. For example, if someone is very cautious and very untrusting as a result of the experiences they had. It's good sense to be like that if you're living in a situation where you're likely to be tortured; it makes really good sense to be hyper-vigilant, to be watchful. It helps you survive.

But it's not useful when you're trying to make new friends, so we try to look at the context of the symptoms.

There are other refugees who just come here and say, 'It's in the past. It's over there and I don't want to talk about it, we don't even talk about it as a family, we don't even talk about it as a couple. There's just no discussion about it. Nothing happened.' And, very often, those are the people who develop nightmares and become quite shocked at the reactions they're having here when they're working so hard to put it away.

Is it difficult to communicate the special problems of refugees to the general public? Is there sometimes confusion about the difference between immigrants and refugees?

I think that there has been an obscuring of it as government policy for a long long time. And I think the Department of Immigration's profile was that these are all immigration issues and that there is no difference between migrants and refugees. What I see is a lot of people being unaware of the difference and that needs to be addressed. People also overlook the strengths and skills refugees bring.

15

Lynne Bon De Veire

When Lynne and I first met, it was in our local park where a number of us walk our dogs. An unofficial 'dog-walking group' was formed where our dogs and children played and fought. What I didn't know in those early days of our friendship was that Lynne had been grieving the death of her young husband, the father of her son.

Lynne is a great cook and one night when she made us dinner she told me the story of her sad loss and the profound journey she has made in trying to make sense of the tragedy. She has known the depth of sadness and is now able to share her insights. It was a moving experience for both of us.

LYNNE BON DE VEIRE

Can you tell me what influenced your husband, Andrew, in making this boat trip?

Andrew saw it as an opportunity of a lifetime. His English father was a submariner, and was all powerful in the family. Andrew didn't see his dad very much, he was always away at sea, interestingly enough. I remember Andrew telling me that when he was five he woke up from a nightmare because he couldn't remember what his father looked like any more. When he did come home, it was a hero's welcome every time. So father was larger than life and he was out there doing dangerous things: the big stuff. I think Andrew's family background and his childhood had a lot to do with Andrew wanting to do something like this—to sail a boat called *Rockin' Robin*—from Sydney to Fiji.

Had he done much boating before?

No. But the older man who owned the boat had sailed the trip before. His son, who was a very good friend of Andrew's, and another friend—all aged thirty-four—were crewing the boat. The father and son were very adventurous. I don't think Andrew was. Andrew was an accountant. He was the quietest, safest boy next-door I'd ever met in my life. So it wasn't as if I'd taken up with an adventurous, risk-taking, bungee-jumping person. Which is why so many of his friends found it really hard to accept what had happened to him, because it was so unlike him to be in a situation like that in the first place.

There was nothing about the way they set out on the trip that was going to endanger them. In fact, the father—who was in his sixties—had said to his wife in the weeks leading up to the trip that he was triple checking everything because he realised the responsibility of taking the three boys away with him. He took it all very seriously.

Was it a big boat?

I'm a complete landlubber, you know. I grew up in Canberra. I only learnt to swim three years ago. All my life I've had a fear of water so I know nothing about sailing boats or any nautical terms or sizes. Andrew did it as a 'boys' own' hobby, he sailed around Pittwater with friends but never any ocean-going sailing. He loved it, found it really exhilarating, but he'd never really bitten off anything big.

So when they invited him to come on and help crew the boat and take it to Noumea and Fiji, he was just beside himself. He told me later that when he heard about it, he worried about whether I'd let him go because Max, our son, was two-and-a-half. It was just bizarre because I'd never say to another adult that they can't do something. You let them know how you feel about it, but when you know how much it means to them, and when they're going to go anyway, then it's enough to say, 'Well, I'm a bit worried about it but if you really want to go, then you must'. Anyhow, none of that even passed my mind.

In the years since then so many women have said to me, 'Why didn't you stop him? Why didn't you tell him he couldn't go?' But I don't have relationships like that. I don't want to be with a man who is going to assume that I'd want to regulate his behaviour. He was very excited about it and he was by nature very cautious anyway. He was probably more worried about it than I was.

Did he express any concerns before he left?

He told me before he went that he knew he was going to be scared out there, but that it was important for him to confront his fear. He was tired of feeling afraid. Not many men have the courage to be that honest. He was at a very important point in his life and was happier and more secure than he'd ever been. He had more to live for—his beautiful baby boy.

Later, when we had to sort out all the paper work and delve into his life, the way you only do when somebody has died, we saw that he had crossed every single 't' and dotted every single 'i' before he left. And the fact that he had been very busy working at night was probably time spent sorting out his personal affairs. The last night he was here we were going out to dinner, but he was late home from work and I was sitting there thinking, 'The last night, and he still can't get home', and I was quite mad. We went to dinner, but by then—I was a young mother—I was passing out at 9 o'clock at night, and I remember sitting down to the meal at 9 o'clock thinking, 'Oh, I want to go home to bed. It's not fair, he comes home late from work and now I'm ready to go to sleep', but it was his last night so we sat and had dinner.

But what he was doing was putting his affairs in order, is that what you mean?

Exactly. He arranged his will and life insurance. Going through the paper work—and it took me years to sort out all the paper work, his personal bills and club memberships et cetera—there was just nothing that hadn't been taken care of. And that is indicative of the fact that he knew he was taking a risk and thought about it very seriously. But that was his nature, to be very thorough and cautious and do all the right things because he was basically a decent human being. A really decent man to his core.

How long was he going to be away?

Three weeks and then we were meant to fly to Fiji to meet him there. He thought he'd tempt me with an airline ticket to Fiji but we were a typical young, struggling family and being the ever-practical person I said, 'No I won't go to Fiji, I'll go to Melbourne and spend a week or two with a close girlfriend there and with the balance of the money for a fare to Fiji, we can buy a washing machine or a fridge. So off you go and have a good time.'

Did you go to see him off?

No. We said good-bye at 7 o'clock in the morning at home. He said good-bye to our son Max and came in and woke me up, because I'd had a late night going to dinner the night before. I heard him getting up and getting ready to go. I said good-bye to him while I was half asleep and he was rushing to jump in the car and go. And I remember feeling a bit hurt. The peculiar thing was, as I heard the front door shut downstairs, out of my mouth came the words, 'Don't go'. Now, normally before you say something you think it, or you think it as you say it, but the words just came out and I thought, 'Oh! Why did I say that? What was that about?' So that was odd.

He sent me a card from Port Stephens to my friend's place in Victoria. I didn't know that they'd been delayed by a day-and-a-half—the customs man who was meant to give them clearance on Monday didn't turn up and they had to re-book for Tuesday.

So you were happily having a holiday with your girlfriend in Victoria, oblivious to what was happening?

Yes. Then on Thursday afternoon Max and I were having an afternoon nap. I woke up feeling quite unsettled and anxious but didn't know why. And Max woke up from his sleep distressed, which was unusual as well because he didn't usually do that. I told my girlfriend that I felt really anxious but didn't know why. I didn't think that there could be anything wrong.

My girlfriend thought it was because we were about to drive into the town to buy food in her two-seater car and we'd had to rig up the baby seat for Max in the back of the car—safely but illegally. We made sure that everything in the car was as safe as it could be because we thought that was what was making me feel anxious.

That feeling stayed with me all day Thursday. On Friday morning I got a phone call at about 10 o'clock from Debbie, the wife of one of the men on board. An aside to this is that Andrew and I were giving up smoking. We thought the fresh sea air might inspire him, and I'd been cutting down to my final cigarette day which was Friday—the day that I was going to become a non-smoker.

Debbie phoned and asked, 'Are you sitting down?' And even then it didn't really register. She said that the yacht had sunk and the boys were in a little bit of trouble, but that Sea Rescue and the RAAF had them in their sights, they were out there, they were doing the rescue mission and that it would only be a matter of time before they were picked up.

Where were they?

They were 500 nautical miles north-east of Queensland, exactly halfway between Noumea and Queensland—couldn't be further away from anything, really, if they tried. I suppose it was partly shock, but I remember the first thing I thought was, 'Where can I get a cigarette?' There were workmen outside so I walked out there, and I remember saying to them quite stupidly, 'Would you mind if I had a few of your cigarettes because my husband's yacht has just sunk and I think I might need a few'.

Debbie had suggested that I might ring Andrew's parents. And that was really the thing that pressed the concern button more than anything—the fact that she felt it was necessary. At that point I started feeling very unwell. I rang his parents. Andrew and his mother were really very close and I couldn't bring myself to tell her directly, so I thought I'd tell his father and he could break the news to her. Debbie had also given me the number for Sea Rescue in Canberra and said that they had a

24-hour hotline to ask about people who were in a state of emergency. So, I immediately rang his parents, then I rang Sea Rescue.

After my first call to them they said, 'Ring any time you want for any reason', so that was good. But I think that they had concluded pretty early that there was no hope for the boys and there was no chance that they'd get them out. But there was a period of time when they needed to be seen to be doing the right thing because their resources were pushed to the limit. It was a really bad unexpected storm, and there were a number of other boats caught in the perimeter of the storm. Our boys were right in the middle.

I think, with their limited resources, they had to choose who they were going to rescue. They pulled out two French women who were on a sailing holiday in the area. In the beginning, though, they were saying that it would only be a matter of time before they pulled our boys out.

And did you feel optimistic at this stage?
Yes. I didn't believe for a long time that anything that major could go wrong in my life because things like that don't happen to me. It was disbelief. My life hadn't been full of death and tragedy or war and trauma and all the things that happen to other people. I knew that it was pretty serious, but I also believe in thinking very positively, so I believed everything was going to be OK.

You thought that they would be pulled out?
Yes. And I remember sitting in a meditative state trying to take it in. Your mind is an amazing thing, it only lets you comprehend a certain amount of a stressful situation at any given time. So I remember sitting thinking, 'It will be all right. It will be all right.' I found myself repeating that in my mind all the time, and sending that out there to Andrew and the boys. And I also remember thinking,

'Andrew, just hang on. Hang on. It will be all right. We'll get you . . . they'll pull you out.'

Was there any radio contact with them?

There was until they got into the raft. There was a mayday call put out on Thursday morning which boats in Botany Bay here in Sydney picked up, and everybody who heard the mayday signal and the following radio communications said that there were certainly no hysterics on board, that the men sounded really calm, capable and competent, but that they knew the boat was sinking.

They didn't report any major damage. The only thing we've been able to work out was that the volume of water which hit the boat was too much for the pump. There was too much water in the boat, basically, and they couldn't get it out. And there must have also been some damage done by the storm to the boat.

We examined photos taken by the RAAF pilot who was the last person to see them alive, and we were in communication with him after the incident as well. He'd taken about ninety black-and-white 10 x 8 photos—a sequential set—showing the boys sailing the yacht towards the raft that the RAAF plane had dropped for them.

So it wasn't a raft from the *Rockin' Robin*?

They had rafts on board, but the severity of the storm just wiped everything out. So they sent out the mayday and the RAAF dropped them a SRK—a Search and Rescue kit—which is two inflatable dinghies joined together by rope that inflate on impact in the water, and a survival kit in between the two rafts. So you'd get in the raft, pull up the cord and get all your provisions. We researched what was in the kits, what they had to eat and what was written on the inside of the raft—the 'how to use' instructions—and they had supplies for two months. The thing that was missing was a tracking device—an EPIRB (Emergency Position Indicating Radio Beacon)—the life or death vital ingredient! The Rescue Kits were not fitted with an EPIRB because, being Navy equipment they're considered unnecessary as all Navy personnel have tracking devices in their life jackets.

They were air-dropped two rescue kits, which means four dinghies altogether. The first two they dropped to them were swept away from the yacht by currents so they dropped them another lot, and then it was slightly off course as well. The sequence of photos shows the boys manoeuvring the yacht, as it was sinking, towards the rafts.

Did they get to the rafts?

Yes, they got to the rafts. We have photos of Andrew. We worked out who was who on the back of the boat, where Grant would be, and where Rob would be, examining the photographs saying, 'That must be Jeff, and that is Andrew', because Andrew's raincoat was 'this' colour and that looked brighter or lighter than the others. So we had photos of them holding onto the raft. The raft is a big inflatable thing with a sort of A-line tent shape over the top of it—unsinkable. You can fill it full of water, you can puncture it, you can do anything to it, we were told, and it would still float on the surface. It could be attacked by frenzied sharks but because of the rubber it's made of, it would still float.

The RAAF pilot said the last time he saw them was at about 5 o'clock on Friday night when he was running out of fuel. So Andrew and the others had been fighting the storm since Thursday morning. On that Friday night at 5 o'clock one or two of them were standing in the raft leaning out of the hatch at the top, and as the plane passed over them they gave the pilot a thumbs up to let him know they were OK. And he gave them a thumbs up, meaning, 'We'll come back and get you'.

When were they to be rescued?

They went out again at first light, in the morning. But by then the boys and the raft weren't where they'd last seen them.

Would they have expected them to be in the same place twelve hours later?

Not in a storm like that. And they also knew there was no tracking device. So Friday night was the last time anybody ever saw them. On Saturday morning they were gone. The boat was gone, there was no trace of anything—nothing—not a skerrick of anything, including three rubber dinghies which were unsinkable. So they are still out there somewhere, they just haven't found them, and they're not looking any more.

Were there any naval vessels available to assist in the search?

There was a French frigate that was literally busting its boiler to get to them, but they were I think a day-and-a-half away when the mayday went out on Thursday. Apparently their engine room was damaged because they were going faster than they should have been going to get there. When they arrived in the general vicinity on Saturday they found one of the dinghies—one of them. When that dinghy was found Search and Rescue said they were calling the search off because there was no one in the dinghy and therefore they must all be lost. The dinghy was taken to the RAAF base in Darwin and when we contacted the base weeks later they had done a forensic report on the dinghy and found that nobody had ever been in it.

Basically, they were running out of resources and they couldn't be seen to be pouring money into something that they considered was a lost cause, but they couldn't actually let us know that. So they said, 'Oh, we've found the dinghy, they're gone so we're calling it off'. So that's when we started searching.

You mounted your own search with private planes and boats?

I'd started to talk to Robin Wiltshire, the skipper's wife, by phone on Saturday. She is an extraordinary woman and I'm very fond of her. My Andrew was like a son to her because she watched him grow up from the time he was a little boy and they were really very fond of each other. I was in contact with her and I'd also spoken to the company Andrew worked for. He had a very strong friendship with one of the key men there, they valued him enormously and wanted him back. So they were fantastic. Robin was just wonderful, she's so full of life and tenacious and doesn't take no for an answer—a woman after my own heart. So I gave Robin the company's number and they got together and talked about doing a search, because Robin kept saying, 'I've got to do something. I can't just leave it like this. There must be something else we can do.' Robin's son was on board too. The search went on for six weeks, every day for six weeks. I spent a lot of time at Robin's house, which was like Command Headquarters. It was a really extraordinary time, like being in a war zone. It was and still is the longest search in Australian maritime history.

There was a lot of media coverage and from that came a lot of public support. We had all the television networks' helicopters flying up to the house to interview us and talk to Robin about what we were doing. There were maps everywhere, there was all this information most of us had never dealt with before.

At the same time as our boys set out on this sailing trip, Robin's son-in-law and members of his family were doing the same trip. They were meant to be making the trip together but they had set sail on schedule, which meant that when the storm hit they were a couple of days ahead. So they were on the perimeter of the storm, on the

Noumea edge. They limped into port, having gone through what they said was the worst storm they had ever seen. The portholes in their yacht were literally punched out of the side of the boat from the severity of the storm and they were two days ahead of where our boys were. So, it was a big one. And, as far as we knew, not forecast.

When they got to Noumea and turned around to say, 'Where are the other guys?', they weren't there. Then they got news that our boys had hit the worst part of the storm. So they flew back immediately and, being sailing people and competent, capable, intelligent people who understood a lot of the information that we were gathering, helped us. Robin understood a lot of it as well because she had sailed before from Port Stephens to Fiji. She's a very boaty, adventurous, larger-than-life woman, and so she and her son-in-law really were the two who started coordinating and assembling all the information. We also had the father of one of the other boys, an ex-RAAF man who gave his expertise. We rang everybody, even the American Embassy in the end, for satellite surveillance, but they said they didn't have a satellite covering that area because it had no significance for them.

We rang the Russians as well to see if they had any surveillance in the area. We rang Dick Smith who was wonderful and donated quite a substantial amount of money to the search. A lot of people just gave, not only financially but everything they could think of to help. I don't remember sleeping, it was just 24-hour days on the phone.

I remember at one point telephoning the Navy to try to get a long-range helicopter. This brings me back to why they didn't airlift the boys out in the beginning—they said it was too rough for a helicopter. But the problem really was that Australia didn't have a helicopter at that time—they were on loan from the Navy. The person I spoke to in the Navy said that they were on loan to the Army who needed them on their peace-keeping mission in Papua New

Guinea and, as far as I know, that's where all of Australia's long-range helicopters are to this day.

We hired private charter planes out of Queensland to search and I think we started out paying something like $250 an hour for a plane to go out, hour after hour after hour. And you know, nothing was every found. A lot of people got on board, people started contacting us and were offering services for various reasons and different fees. The money initially, I think, came from the company Andrew was working for. And then the insurance company that Robin's boat was insured with agreed to release the money for the boat so that it could be put towards the search.

We contacted people in Papua New Guinea because we had experts calling us for weeks saying, 'There are currents in that part of the sea at this time of the year and they'll end up at the mouth of the Fly River, so that's where you've got to look. You've got to go "up here". You've got to go "over there" . . .'

We had clairvoyants ringing us telling us they knew where they were. It was amazing, people just came out of the woodwork. It was just extraordinary, the amount of support we received.

Robin was on television at one point and the program was inundated with people calling to offer support. People wrote to Robin via newspapers, we had endless letters from people whom we'd never met and would never meet, just telling us to keep going and offering support. Robin has folders full of correspondence from people we've never known. And a lot of really touching stories from people who had been through extraordinary things themselves who wrote, 'My own regret was that I'd never done enough at the time', or, 'that I hadn't followed through', and we said to each other that we had to try everything that we could think of, because we have the rest of our lives to live with it.

It would take volumes to recount what happened

during those six weeks. We had so much evidence, hundreds of phone calls came in, retired navy admirals giving us expertise and hope. There were dozens of people at Robin's house on 24-hour shifts. We were all fed and cared for in the most extraordinary way—picked up when we fell down, and always waiting for THE phone call . . .

It was impossible to just let it lie. It would have eaten us away. And we all felt a very strong degree of anger toward the government and Sea Rescue because there was a lot of evidence pointing to negligence.

Was that ever proven?

Well, they completely reorganised the department after our incident, and the Minister in charge was shifted sideways. There was no senior officer on duty the night that the major decisions were made, they were understaffed. Robin was in correspondence with the powers that be for years after the *Rockin' Robin* event and they wrote to let her know of changes they'd made within the department, and thanked her for her concern and support in trying to facilitate a more efficient set-up.

So it was an admission that things weren't running efficiently.

Absolutely. There was also a really extraordinary man involved in all of this who came in about halfway through. Robin and I had been given his name separately by different people. He's a QC, Laurie Gruzman, who is from time to time in the news, most often about Search and Rescue—it's been his passion for years—Search and Rescue in Australia and internationally: the equipment they use everywhere else in the world, and the equipment that our government continues to resist purchasing. The equipment is available locally, proven to be superior (that is, lifesaving) and endorsed by almost everyone interested in this area. Anyone who saw *Sixty Minutes* on 9 June (which was the sixth anniversary of our boys' disappearance) would know that this is still a very urgent issue, all these years later. What will they do when thousands of people go sailing in the year 2000? Maybe we should put rescue equipment on to the Olympic budget.

Laurie actually flew for us for weeks and weeks, free of charge . . . a QC, a very busy man. He was very involved in our case and in there boots and all. He did extraordinary things for us. At the end of the search, there were a lot of questions unanswered. There was a case to answer. The government held their own inquiry into the sinking of the *Rockin' Robin*, which didn't show them in a favourable way. There has been talk of litigation, but our babies have lost their dads, we decided that they shouldn't also lose their mums for however many years the case would require.

Given all the information you have from that time, what do you think actually happened?

We were told that if the raft turned over it could be righted from the inside. So, we were told that they could get into the raft, strap themselves in and they had enough provisions for two months. In a rough sea if the raft flipped over there was enough head airspace in the upturned raft, even when it was full of water, so you wouldn't drown if you were inside the raft. And from there, if you did certain things you could right it. The RAAF pilot who saw them all day Friday said that he saw the raft go over a couple of times as he passed them by, and he saw them out in the water righting it each time. He said that it was pretty rough and wondered, 'God, I wonder how many times they'll be able to do that—they're exhausted'.

They had life jackets—civilian, not Navy issue. But we were told that the wind was so strong that, even if they could float with their heads well above water, the volume of spray in the air would drown them. So, which way do you face to keep the spray out of your face in a cyclone?

I don't know. Apparently it was one notch below a cyclone.

When I went to bed that Friday night, my girlfriend was just extraordinary. I couldn't have been with a better person at the time. She went to the local doctor and talked to him. There was some Valium in the house. I didn't want to take them but we agreed that I needed to get some sleep, so I think I took half a Valium which made me feel a lot better, it just calmed me a bit. And I remember, for about three or four days, her feeding me and coming with cups of tea and making me drink while I was on the phone. I remember spending a week out in the corridor. It was winter and the floor in the house was centrally heated but the corridor where the phone was, near the kitchen, wasn't. So I was wrapped up in doonas with a box of tissues on one side and a pile of Wet Ones on the other, and being brought brown rice and parsley, because I couldn't eat anything, and tea. Every now and again she'd literally come in and unwrap me and pick me up, physically drag me to my feet and take me into the bedroom and put me to bed. She did that for days. I can't imagine going through something like that if you had nobody else in the world.

When did you come to accept the fact that Andrew had died?

When Helen put me to bed that Friday night she said, 'Just be with him. Just lie down and put yourself out there with him. Just be there and tell him that it will be all right. Just keep telling him that'. So, that's what I did.

I remember lying down—Max and I were sharing a king-size bed—and I put his hand on the pillow with my thumb in his tiny hand. As I was going to sleep and I was imagining being out there with Andrew and saying, 'It will be all right. It will be all right', the pillow became Andrew for me, as I drifted off into sleep.

I could subconsciously hear, because I was putting myself out there with him, the noise of the storm—and this is where it gets hard—I could hear this incredible noise in my head of the storm, and I started to think how frightened he must have been. The hardest part was thinking about how he felt knowing that he might not see Max again. That is absolutely the hardest part for me. Knowing that he had to go through feeling that for however long before he died. The anxiety involved knowing that you're leaving a child behind, to me is just unbearable pain. And the fact that it was happening to him—somebody I knew and loved. So, that was really difficult.

And then at 6 o'clock on Saturday morning I was wide awake and thought, 'Oh, no, why am I awake . . .', the worst part about being in shock and in grief is that every time you wake up, you remember again. You have a split second as you come out of sleep where things could be quite normal, and then it hits you again. I can understand why people don't want to go to sleep or can't go to sleep, or want to go to sleep and never wake up. It's the severity of the shock that continues to hit you, you don't just have one shock and then start to recover, you have a shock every time.

I'd got up to go to the toilet, and when I got back into bed I started feeling really distressed and thought, 'I'll do what Helen told me to do last night, and I'll just lie here and be with him and tell him it will be all right', so I was doing that. And as I lay there the noise of the storm was all around. Then gradually I had this feeling of floating. I was floating up and Andrew's chest was right under my face, and I was saying, 'It will be all right. It will be all right', and I realised that we weren't in the raft together anymore. I realised that the raft was gone and it was getting further and further and further away, and as the raft got further away, the noise of the storm was abating as well, it was getting quieter and quieter and we were floating up-up-up . . . and it was warm and quiet. And then I drifted off into sleep.

I knew that it was him going—at 6 o'clock that Saturday morning. But I didn't want to really accept it. I was still in Torquay and I had to get back to Sydney. There was a search to be done. But that is what I feel happened, that he drowned at 6 o'clock Saturday morning having fought the storm for two days. About a year after the search, Robin and I were having dinner one night and I told her of that experience and when I thought that Andrew had died.

She said, 'Well, I never would have believed that Andrew would have lasted longer than my boys'. I said, 'What do you mean?' And she replied, 'Well, I'm not sure which one it was, but one of mine went at 4 o'clock on Saturday morning'. We both felt it was amazing . . . that Andrew who was less adventurous but strong . . . and Robin said, 'It shows how much he loved you and Max that he hung in there that long'.

So that is when I think he died. But we searched for six weeks . . . we had to do that.

Can you tell me about your relationship with Andrew?

It was built on love and respect and trust . . . a level of trust that neither of us had had before. And I think it was quite a rare thing. There was a lot of understanding. It was a very profound and rewarding relationship for both of us because we worked at it. We worked very hard at it, because we started out respecting each other and that was where we wanted to end up. No matter what happened we needed to maintain that respect. And we learnt a lot about ourselves and about each other. It was a very profound relationship.

And Andrew adored our son Max. He was a gentle and loving father. He, like most young dads, was very intense about the career part of his life, so that was often difficult to juggle. But Andrew grew up with a father who was often away, and he said to me that as he grew up he had made a promise to himself that if ever he was going to have a child, he would not be an absent father because he was aware of the effect that had had on him.

He was a very family-oriented person, had a warm, affectionate relationship with his mother and brother and sister. He had very firm and slightly old-fashioned family values. He wanted to be there for Max. So, this is all a little ironic now that he's gone.

What does the concept of 'recovery' from grief mean to you?

The one thing about being in a state of grief that strikes me as being a little peculiar is that it's one of the most profound states to be in. And society generally has this concept that it should be a phase that has a beginning and an end, and that you should get over it. And we don't have that expectation about any other feeling that we have in our lives, except grief and sadness. We don't feel comfortable with people who are sad. And 'sad' is the word that kept cropping up for me when I was coming to terms with this.

It just kept striking me how it's one of the biggest words in the entire English language, yet it only has three letters. 'Sad' is the only way to describe it when every cell in your body aches, and it still doesn't really sum it up. People come up with millions of words for states of being, none of them really describes it properly, but 'sad' is the one that I kept coming back to.

Recovery for me is learning how to live with that sadness. It becomes a part of who we are. So I don't know if 'recovery' is a term I'd use. It felt more like absorbing a set of circumstances and learning to live with it within myself, within my own head and body.

I think, when people are put into this kind of situation, shock is a wonderful thing because it cushions you from the gravity of the situation. Even though what you've experienced is so overwhelming that the most obvious emotion is fear—'I can't feel all of this. I don't want to look at it. I can't deal with it. I can't cope. I'll try to be strong . . .' all these things to me are to do with fear of allowing yourself to feel. What I found is that I should have trusted my body and my mind more than I did. But the fear of going into that place in my emotions where I'd never been before, and being fearful of being there in case I didn't come back out, was very real.

I think most people grow up with an extraordinary level of fear about everything, from being out at night on your own, getting sick and so on. Being afraid of being left alone.

And when we're presented with a situation like this, everything becomes more extreme. It's being on another planet, it's being somewhere else. I felt I floated in ether for about eighteen months after Andrew died. I was somewhere between Earth and what I conceptualised as Heaven, because it was a comfort zone. I floated between the two.

I was nurtured by an incredible number of wonderful people who cushioned me from a lot of the realities that one normally has to deal with in life. I don't believe that people can live with that level of distress, sadness, fear and loss and not be ill unless they have help to deal with it. Because none of us is taught how to deal with any of those emotions other than to be afraid of them.

To me, fear can be healthy because it's what keeps us alive if we're under attack—the fear is what sets us going and it's our survival instinct. But I think everybody carries around so much of it. I'm a great believer in fate and if things are meant to happen, they're meant to happen. And every person you come across, you meet for a reason.

I'd been told about the Bereavement Care Centre and I'm a firm believer in speaking to somebody objective in times of extreme stress—whether it's marital or to do with your children or other important issues.

With grief and loss, there is a very strong innate mechanism to spare your friends from the distress that you feel. If they knew how bad I felt after six months, they would have been devastated and I didn't want to do that to them.

So I felt relieved that there was somewhere I could go to talk to someone. The thing that was most important for me about the Centre was that you walk in there and you feel it's a safe place to be, at a purely subconscious level, it's a safety zone. And it is that in all senses of the word.

So bereavement counselling was important to you.

It was the beginning of the process of learning how to live with what had happened. I can't say enough good things about the Centre. Other people have been to different counsellors and therapists to help them deal with their issues of grief, often recommended by the family doctor, but I believe that it probably doesn't hit the mark. I think what the Bereavement Care Centre have set up is truly extraordinary. And, of course, they're international leaders in this field, with good reason. The counsellor assigned to me was just perfect. We have had further contact recently, which is a joy.

The level of professionalism and ethics in there is exemplary. The training that they go through is pretty rugged, to say the least. Judy, my counsellor, said that the reason she enjoyed specialising in the area of bereavement was that you got people without any bullshit at all. Most other therapies, psychotherapies and counselling work, are to do with peeling away the layers of defences that people have, but when you're in a state of bereavement, you're in a really primal state of sheer terror and fear. While people around you are making cups of tea and bringing in meals and asking how you are today and you're saying, 'I'm OK this afternoon, I had a bad morning, but this afternoon is OK', inside you are probably more terrified of everything than you've ever been before.

So in that state of fear and excruciating distress, you go in to a place that is safe and you deal with somebody who understands totally why and what you are experiencing. The first couple of sessions I went in and just cried for hours. She said to me that our society doesn't mark grief the way other societies do by wearing black armbands or wearing black. We don't mark it at all.

One of the marks of grief within the Centre, we both noticed, was the obligatory box of tissues in every room—large boxes of tissues—and I'd always end up with a mountain of absolutely sodden tissues. If ever you felt shy about crying in front of anybody, just forget it! Judy said she thought we should mark our grief by wearing a white towel over one shoulder to sob into, because tissues are totally inadequate.

But with weeping of such depth and magnitude, I thought 'I'm never going to get up'. There were times I ended up on the floor. I'd literally just flop onto the floor. I didn't have the strength to sit up in the chair. And Judy would just sit with me . . . she never came over and put her arm around my shoulder and said, 'There, there dear, you'll feel better', which is the instinct that your friends have. That then makes you feel responsible for the fact that they're trying to make you feel better . . . therefore you have to pull yourself together quicker. Whereas this set-up enables you to weep and weep, and you know that if you are going into that black hole you've been terrified of all your life, the person who is sitting in the room with you is equipped to know when you're going in there, and how to pull you back out again, and how to keep you safe.

You know that if you fall down on the ground and weep until your body literally just falls apart—which is how it feels—that if you pass out you're still going to be all right, because the person in the room with you can deal with it.

What was the turning point for you?
I realised that I had cried as much as I could. I didn't feel that I was holding on to anything. I wasn't trying to be

better or brave or strong . . . And the sense of liberty and freedom that comes with that is one of the best things about this whole life episode. Coming face-to-face with your fears and your depth of feeling, to do with every single thing that has ever made you feel sad in your entire life. Because I have a really strong feeling that grief is cumulative.

When I was at the Centre in counselling, I thought, 'I feel so lucky that I'm doing this now', because I was dumping thirty-four years of grief and distress. It wasn't just Andrew going, it was everything and they know that as well, you can't have one without the other—it's everything to do with your life.

A lot of people don't have that opportunity to do that. I've never felt lighter or freer, and to me this is one of the gifts that Andrew has given me by going off and dying on me.

And it's to do with saying everything you want to say about the loss. Thinking doesn't do your body any good at the end of the day. Thinking something over and over again that you might not feel good about, doesn't do your health a great deal of good. Saying these things openly to another human being, in a totally protected and discreet environment, means you can put it down. You can pick it up and put it 'over there'. You take it off your chest . . . you know, all the cliches and analogies are valid for a reason. It's over there and it's no longer in your body. And in my case I didn't know whether Andrew was dead or not, he just simply disappeared . . .

Being able to go through the process of saying, 'I am so afraid that if I feel this deeply I might never recover. I am so afraid that if I never see Andrew again, I'll never be able to say certain things to him. My deepest fear about what this means for Max is . . .' Verbalising that was the beginning of saying goodbye.

I'm not saying everybody needs grief in their life to get a sense of what life is about, but at some point we have to come face-to-face with it. About a year later we had a memorial service for Andrew. Many people had asked if there would be one. It's very important to mark it in some way. Rituals are a vital part of putting something to rest. His disappearance devastated many lives. We all still miss him terribly.

I think one of the first things that you need to do when you go into shock and grief is to get rid of the word, 'should'. Every time you feel yourself thinking, 'I should', get rid of it. But at the same time increase your awareness of your levels of security and well being, in a sense that yes, you should eat and, yes, you should get out of bed and, yes, you should shower and you should leave the house. And if you're fortunate enough to have people around you who are going to watch out for you, then in your head you can stop thinking, 'I should see my friend because she wants to come and help me feel better'. If you don't want to see your friend, have the strength to say, 'I don't want to see you right now'.

And this is also where people say you sort out who your friends are, because a real friend will accept that you need to be left alone maybe for six months, and then one day they'll call you. I had friends who rang every couple of weeks and my sister bought me an answering machine which was indispensable. I didn't have to answer the phone. I had messages coming in from people saying they're just thinking about me . . . and that was important to hear.

In what ways has your life changed since Andrew died?
In every way—profoundly. Some good, some less so. Andrew died when I was thirty-four. That's six years ago. I am now forty and forty is fabulous. Being on my own at thirty-four with a two-and-a-half-year-old child, I was busy being a single mum and adjusting. Being on my own has taught me a lot about myself. I think people don't spend enough time on their own.

And again, being a fatalist I think I am on my own

for a reason, because there are things that I need to learn from this. And, you know, it's wonderful to find out that the really shitty mood you're in is because it's your shit and nobody else's! So, it's all to do with living on your own and not being lonely. Living on your own but being interested in yourself, not in a self-absorbed way, but interested in what you can learn and achieve and what you can glean from it.

Part of me has felt the need to scurry away, in the sense that I think being out there in the world the way I was, most of my working life, required a certain level of energy and aggression, and I feel that I have a very, very full-time job being a single parent. And, you know, the great misunderstood people of our society are single parents. Unless you're a single parent you really don't know what it's like. But that is my most important job.

I've been very lucky in that Andrew was very thorough tying up loose ends in his life, because he was that sort of person. It has enabled me to be there for Max. Now, that's a very, very fortunate position to be in because it means that Max lost one parent and not two. And I think there should be a special bereavement allowance paid to any single parent. You can lose one, but losing two is what happens most of the time. So, yes, it's been very fortunate for both Max and me.

Tell me about Max.

He's eight-and-a-half now and I've been profoundly in love with him since the day he was born. He is the most beautiful boy in the entire world. He has his dad's long legs, his hands and feet. His dad's full lips and his nose. It's wonderful to see Andrew in him. I think he'll grow up to be quite like him as well. He's an excellent communicator and languages come naturally to him. He's got a great ear for music, too, and knows our CD library very well. He knows exactly when to put on Bach's Cello

Suites, to 'chill Mum out'. He's also extremely energetic, and sensitive at the same time.

Can you tell me about your work?
I design and make clothes for women, and I love what I do, most of the time anyway. I've had creative jobs most of my life and this is an extension of it. To make something for somebody to put on and go somewhere for a special occasion, or to just wear because it's the most comfortable thing they've got, to me is like cooking a good meal for somebody—it's a sensory experience.

Most of the people I work for are friends as well as clients. I think I'm lucky to be able to do this because it's part of a dream, an idea of what I wanted to do with my life.

I love textiles. I designed textiles in Como in Italy for a couple of years, and I've worked in and out of the rag trade between Italy and here. It's mainly around the Italian silk industry where I left part of my heart. So I love good textiles. I've not had any formal training to do what I'm doing, but being able to think three dimensionally when you're designing something apparently is a valuable asset. Others work things out on paper in two dimensions whereas I do all my designing with my eyes closed, and that's the only way I can work.

I love the contact with people but I also need to spend time just sitting quietly working, which is what my job enables me to do. I have the most exquisite music going in my studio all day long. I especially love cello music. and I make myself a fabulous lunch.

A couple of years ago I discovered the viola da gamba—the instrument before the cello. I feel more passionately about cellos, cello music and viola da gamba music than I have about any other music. I narrowly missed out on having piano lessons when I was a teenager and after Andrew died I thought, Gosh, I could be really depressed by the time I'm forty. I've spent years on my own being a single parent, driving my friends nuts because I'm going to be a bit of a weight for a while, and I hope I don't feel really unloved and left behind when I am turning forty or my life could be very bloody sad indeed. So I thought, 'I'd better start thinking about it now. What can I do? What can I do to start looking forward to being 40?'

About five years ago I thought, 'Maybe I ought to take up the piano. What a good idea.' I went through the process of where I'd find one, and where I'd put it and what fun it would be to have a musical instrument in the house, because I've not had one before. And then a girlfriend was given a cello and she and another friend who has a cello came to my house for New Year's lunch one day in my garden. It was summer. They both sat there with their cellos—neither of them could play. One of them had had a few lessons but the other one hadn't started and they sat and mucked about. We all fell about laughing because it was just a wonderful thing to do.

I love the look of them. I love everything about cellos. I just looked at my friends sitting there in the garden in the sun and it filled me with joy. Anyone who has ever fallen in love with the cello will probably know exactly what I mean.

That was the first time I'd picked up a cello. I sat and bowed a few times. And I thought, 'Why am I thinking of a piano?' So I started cello lessons and it's one of the most wonderful things that I've ever done in my life.

So between your work and your boy Max and the cello, it sounds to me as if your life is very busy.

I love my life most of the time. I still have bad days and, like everyone, I get tired and cranky sometimes, but I look after myself physically very well. I go to yoga, an absolute must for physical recovery. I swim in summer, which was a new thing. I'd spent all my life being terrified of water because I never ever swam as a child, and suddenly there

I was—Andrew had died by drowning, all my greatest fears had come true and I still couldn't swim. So three years after he died I went for swimming lessons with Max and we learnt how to swim together. I still am not 100 per cent sure about water but that's been a wonderful, liberating thing to do.

And I move around in my studio at home working, listening to music. It would be nice to share it. I do share it with friends. I don't have someone special in my life but I have the knowledge that I was the most wonderful human being in the world for Andrew, and he told me that before he went. He sat me down and said a lot of things to me just before he went. And what he said to me has helped me cope with him not being here with me any more.

What did he say?

He thanked me for Max and he said, 'You're the only woman I want to be with, and I'll love you more than any other woman till the day I die'. And that was the most fabulous thing he could have said before he went, because that's all anybody really wants to hear. I think you're very lucky if you have that once in your life.

16

Dianne McKissock

Dianne McKissock OAM is a Director of the Bereavement Care Centre. She has trained as a sociologist, a marriage and family therapist, psychotherapist and bereavement counsellor. She has worked as a therapist for the past twenty-six years. She and her husband, Mal McKissock, established the Bereavement Care Centre ten years ago.

Dianne, what are the major signposts in recovery from the death of a spouse or a loved one?

Often it's a movement from 'self' focus to 'other' focus. And grief is incredibly self-focused. I hesitated about saying 'self-centred' because that always sounds a critical thing to say. It's just that when we're grieving it affects every part of our being, so we really don't have much choice about being self-focused.

It's hard to be terribly concerned about anything else that's going on when your whole priority is focused on your own survival. But as your needs begin to be met by the environment, the change that occurs is in becoming aware of the environment again and people in the environment.

So, as a counsellor, for instance, I might notice that my client is telling me of their concerns about other people, their family, or they might start to notice things about me as a person.

What is the time frame, and what stages do people go through in their grief?

We no longer talk about stages—that's a concept that became very familiar to people via Kubler-Ross some years ago and was used really for teaching purposes to describe what happened to people after the diagnosis of a terminal illness. It wasn't really meant to be applied to people who are grieving or bereaved.

The 'stage' concept got taken on rigidly by people because it was something that was concrete. Most people felt so helpless and anxious around grief that when there seemed to be a clear framework they reached out and clung onto that like a life raft, but we no longer talk about stages because that's not how it happens.

More accurately, it's related to theories of chaos rather than any 'stage' kind of model. Grief is just all over the place, and the emotional and physical response to grief will continue in some degree, in some form, for the rest of the person's life. So in terms of a time frame, here we would talk about new grief as being within the first two years.

Grief is a major crisis in our lives. Because of this, most people dealing with it from a therapeutic perspective have used a crisis model, and when you're working with a crisis model you're looking at short-term interventions, often over a six to twelve week period. Crisis has its major impact in the first six to twelve weeks.

The general community's perception was that we would recover from the grief in that same kind of time frame, and it doesn't happen. It can't. It's too big a crisis, it impacts too much on every aspect of our being. So we changed even the words we use, and talked about it as being new grief for the first two years rather than the crisis period.

But it may take people up to five years to regain the level of meaning in their life they had prior to that death. That doesn't mean they're going to spend every minute of the five years feeling totally miserable. There's a fluctuating range of emotions that occurs in different time frames in that period. But we don't consider it unusual for it to take up to five years for someone to again feel that life has a desirable level of meaning.

And what happens within that time frame? What are the emotions that one would expect to experience?

It differs from person to person. It is determined by things like the kinds of emotions that were modelled or acceptable in our family of origin and our gender—for instance, males are more likely to express anger around grief, and females are more likely to express sadness.

There's an expectation in the community, I think, partly because of that 'stage' model of grief, that everyone goes through a stage of anger, whereas some people never feel angry around grief, they just feel sad. Fear is a part of it—fear of a whole range of things, and that might be from mild anxiety to full-scale panic attacks. And it's also going to be influenced by age, physical health, previous life history. If people have had a series of other losses in their lives which are still affecting them in a pronounced way, then this current loss is going to impact differently.

Any psychological problems they might have had in the past—drug and alcohol use and so on—are going to influence the kind of emotions that are felt and how they are shown. But for most people there's an intense, what we would call passionate sadness, which is often mistakenly labelled depression, and that's of concern. For us it's fairly easy to differentiate between depression and passionate sadness. But the general community doesn't do that so readily, and that includes the medical profession.

As a consequence, people are often medicated inappropriately.

Most people would at some point feel some kind of shock or numbness—not in the clear sequential way that might have been talked about in earlier times. They might have recurring feelings of numbness and I think that's a protection against the onslaught of emotions. We can only stand so much for a certain period of time, then numbing ourselves becomes an effective defence.

How do we deal with grief compared to other cultures? Are there other societies which deal with death and grieving more effectively?

I think at first glance, a number of other cultures appear to. They do some things better than we do. For instance, they might have rituals that are more effective and there is more permission for overt expression at a funeral in a number of other cultures.

In our culture we do bizarre things like drugging people to get them through the funeral. The funeral is supposed to be something that facilitates grief and it should be the one place where you can make as much noise as you want, express all the passionate feeling that you have. But people feel they have to maintain an appearance that satisfies others.

We're supposed to be stoic.

Very stoic. We've got very English influences in that sense. So the more stoic we are the more praise and support we're likely to receive from those around us. And we conform to that because we're so vulnerable and terrified of losing anyone else, we do things to please people. In that sense I think there are many cultures which do better in terms of their rituals and their permission for weeping and wailing.

Even doing things like wearing black clothing and black armbands must have been an important part of the ritual, but it's not very common now.

I think that sort of ritual was very important. Things that said to people, 'I hurt. Treat me gently.' There's a definite place for the return of that sort of thing. In some cultures they wear red and in some it's white. But to wear something that says, 'I hurt', I think is a reasonable thing.

Why is it that some people recover from a bereavement better than others? Some go on to live a new and satisfying life, while others simply don't.

There are a number of risk factors that we've identified, so if there are two or more of those present, they have the potential to complicate grief. They are factors such as the suddenness of the death; the death of a child; preventability; the degree of centrality of the deceased—how central that person was in the bereaved person's life; a decrease in the roles that they might now be able to fulfil. For instance, if a mother has a young child die and that child is the focus of her love, then she's not only lost her child but she's lost her reason for being—her identity. It was her major role and where most of her energy was focused.

Lack of social support. Pre-existing psycho-pathology. Unresolved losses from the past. Drug and alcohol use. Lack of reality when there's no access to a body after death—if someone dies and the body isn't found. Or caring relatives and friends who prevent someone spending time with that person after they've died, wanting to save them an experience that's distressing. There's no sense of reality in that situation. All these are risk factors.

If there's a loving support system around you and you're given permission to be yourself, not to grieve the way someone else does or the way someone thinks you ought to, if that's facilitated it assists in the process. And it helps if you're allowed to talk about the person who has died as much as you need until you build a new relationship with that person.

Part of what we do wrong is to encourage people to let go, to separate themselves from the person who has died. But we instinctively know that's not what we're meant to do. You're never meant to let go. The person dies but the relationship doesn't. And a lot of what we've done to grieving people in the past is to encourage them to put it behind them, get on with life . . . almost forget about it.

We've said critical things like, 'Well, you've got to let so-and-so, go', rather than letting them talk about it over and over until they move from that external relationship to building a relationship that's internal—where they have the confidence that they can retain that connection. We help them reconnect with the dead person so they have confidence about keeping that connection for the rest of their life. It's crucial not to take the connection away from them. That is one of the factors that leads to a good outcome.

Support, and being given a role, being able to be oneself, those kinds of things are crucial. If you've grown up in a family where your needs haven't been met, if you haven't had sufficient nurturing as a child and there are deficits in that childhood background, that is going to affect the way you respond to current stressors or to current grief. If you've been abused as a child and if your trust has been damaged, that's certainly going to affect the outcome. So nurturing deficits and childhood abuse are among the biggest contributing factors to a negative outcome.

Perhaps the term recovery isn't, in fact, appropriate. Is adjustment a better description?

You're right in thinking that. The word that we use more commonly now is accommodation . . . that you learn to accommodate this experience into the totality of your life. To include it rather than to recover from it. You would have found talking to all the people you've interviewed that when you have a major loss in your life you never forget it, you never 'get over it', as people expect. You learn to live with it.

What you're grappling with, as a bereaved person and with the people around you, is helplessness. Your ideas, your illusions about life have been confronted . . . your illusion about being in control. So as a bereaved person we learn that we can't control outcomes. The people who care about us, who are helpless to control the effect that it's having on us, often do things which aren't terribly helpful from that position of helplessness, like trying to distract when distraction isn't the best thing at a particular time. Each one of us has to develop a rhythm of contact and withdrawal from our pain. There's a rhythm that we've learnt in our families of origin about that—of how long each individual in the family can tolerate emotional pain.

But eventually our lives can be as rich, or in some instances even richer, when we've finally accommodated the death of someone close to us.

Yes. Life returns to a new kind of normal. Priorities may have changed, old friendships been questioned or new ones formed, and our sense of security and control challenged. But all this may be balanced by a more passionate appreciation of life with all its uncertainty and fragility, and a determination to live life more fully now. I think that the ability to survive the initial helplessness of bereavement, to accommodate the pain of loss into our lives, is a very grown up thing to do. It has the potential to be empowering.

MORE GOOD BOOKS FROM ALLEN & UNWIN

THE RESILIENT SPIRIT

Transforming suffering into insight, compassion and renewal

POLLY YOUNG-EISENDRATH

We all go through hard times in our lives, but most of us try to avoid the pain and suffering they bring. We forget that suffering is not only an essential part of being human, but is also a powerful teacher with the potential to bring strength and wisdom.

Drawing on the traditions that have enriched her own life experience—the teachings of Buddhism, the thinking of Carl Jung and the practice of psychoanalysis—Polly Young-Eisendrath illuminates the lives of four people who have faced tremendous hardships, yet found renewed insight and compassion as a result. Their stories allow us to explore our own experiences in a meaningful context, to be guided through the fundamental transition from suffering to compassion and, ultimately, from pain to transformation.

The Resilient Spirit is a constructive and companionable guide to the path of spiritual growth.

1 86448 372 5

MORE GOOD BOOKS FROM ALLEN & UNWIN

ONE IN 10

Women living with breast cancer

DIANA WARD

'I keep wanting to say to people who hear about my cancer that I'm no less alive and vital now. I have more if anything to give to others. They mustn't walk away from me or feel I'm contagious or love me any less.'

'I thought life was a struggle but since I've been forced to let go of so much, I've discovered life is easy and joyful.'

What is it like to know that you have breast cancer? The women in this book answer that often unspoken question, with wit, fortitude, passion and humour. Their experience of this disease varies widely—there are no simple recipes for recognising it, preventing it, treating it or overcoming fear of it, but what stands out in all the stories is how resolved and altered each woman is as a result; not one remains self-pitying and many see the experience as having a profoundly creative effect on their lives.

Despite the sorrow and suffering, *One in 10* reveals women who are dealing, each in her own way, with dilemmas which confront every woman living with breast cancer in the 1990s.

1 86448 037 8